DECORATING
SMALL SPACES

Better Homes and Gardens® Books | Des Moines, Iowa

BETTER HOMES AND GARDENS. BOOKS
AN IMPRINT OF MEREDITH. BOOKS

▶ **DECORATING SMALL SPACES**
EDITOR Vicki L. Ingham
CONTRIBUTING EDITOR AND PROJECT WRITER Shelley Stewart
SENIOR ASSOCIATE DESIGN DIRECTOR Doug Samuelson
GRAPHIC DESIGN Beth Runcie, Conyers Design, Inc.
COPY CHIEF Terri Fredrickson
COPY AND PRODUCTION EDITOR Victoria Forlini
EDITORIAL OPERATIONS MANAGER Karen Schirm
MANAGERS, BOOK PRODUCTION Pam Kvitne, Marjorie J. Schenkelberg, Rick von Holdt
CONTRIBUTING COPY EDITOR Ro Sila
CONTRIBUTING PROOFREADERS Kathi Di Nicola, Sue Fetters, David Krause
INDEXER Beverley Nightenhelser
EDITORIAL AND DESIGN ASSISTANTS Kaye Chabot, Karen McFadden, Mary Lee Gavin

▶ **MEREDITH® BOOKS**
EDITOR IN CHIEF Linda Raglan Cunningham
DESIGN DIRECTOR Matt Strelecki
EXECUTIVE EDITOR, HOME DECORATING AND DESIGN Denise L. Caringer

PUBLISHER James D. Blume
EXECUTIVE DIRECTOR, MARKETING Jeffrey Myers
EXECUTIVE DIRECTOR, NEW BUSINESS DEVELOPMENT Todd M. Davis
EXECUTIVE DIRECTOR, SALES Ken Zagor
DIRECTOR, OPERATIONS George A. Susral
DIRECTOR, PRODUCTION Douglas M. Johnston
BUSINESS DIRECTOR Jim Leonard

VICE PRESIDENT AND GENERAL MANAGER Douglas J. Guendel

▶ **BETTER HOMES AND GARDENS® MAGAZINE**
EDITOR IN CHIEF Karol DeWulf Nickell
DEPUTY EDITOR, HOME DESIGN Oma Blaise Ford

▶ **MEREDITH PUBLISHING GROUP**
PRESIDENT, PUBLISHING GROUP Stephen M. Lacy
VICE PRESIDENT-PUBLISHING DIRECTOR Bob Mate

▶ **MEREDITH CORPORATION**
CHAIRMAN AND CHIEF EXECUTIVE OFFICER William T. Kerr

IN MEMORIAM E. T. Meredith III (1933-2003)

All of us at Better Homes and Gardens. Books are dedicated to providing you with information and ideas to enhance your home. We welcome your comments and suggestions. Write to us at: Better Homes and Gardens Books, Home Decorating and Design Editorial Department, 1716 Locust St., Des Moines, IA 50309-3023.

If you would like to purchase any of our home decorating and design, cooking, crafts, gardening, or home improvement books, check wherever quality books are sold. Or visit us at: bhgbooks.com

I think that the term "small space" is relative to your changing needs and expectations. My own definition has changed many times over the years. On moving day my first house seemed like a giant empty space with large rooms clamoring for furniture to fill them. Later, after my second child was born, that same house suddenly was much too small to accommodate my family and furnishings.

We temporarily crammed ourselves into an apartment while we were building our spacious dream house. Later, when a job in another city beckoned, we relocated to another apartment (the largest that we could find, but far smaller than either the house we had left or the one we later bought). Since then I've had several houses, each with more space in some areas, less space in others. And I, design-conscious soul that I am, have been determined to decorate each place so that it lived like a true home and not a temporary way station. How I wish that I could have had a book like this to help me make the most of whatever space we had, instead of finding my own way by trial and error and learning through costly mistakes!

In this book you will learn simple, space-enhancing principles and see how they work in rooms and whole houses. Information on color and pattern, arrangement and scale, and clever storage ideas will help you with the basics. You'll also learn to fool the eye with illusion, to convert furniture or rooms for alternate uses, and to make smarter use of existing space. Then, no matter what its size, you'll know how to create a home that lives larger and looks more lovely. ◀

Shelley Stewart

chapter one
PRINCIPLES

CONTENTS

Learn simple guidelines for decorating, and your small spaces will seem larger and function better.

8 ▸ Color & Pattern

20 ▸ Arrangement & Scale

28 ▸ Storage

38 ▸ Illusion

58 ▸ Conversions

68 ▸ Smart Use of Space

chapter two
ROOM BY ROOM

chapter three
WHOLE HOUSES

Use space-enhancing principles to bring out the full decorative potential of every room in your home.

Create a space-savvy home that reflects your personal tastes by using tried-and-true principles.

80 ▶ Living Rooms

88 ▶ Dining Areas

98 ▶ Kitchens

108 ▶ Bedrooms & Baths

122 ▶ Workstations

130 ▶ Found Spaces

140 ▶ Young Modern

148 ▶ Offbeat Traditional

156 ▶ Artful Contemporary

164 ▶ Heirloom Cottage

170 ▶ Urban Elegance

178 ▶ Easygoing Eclectic

184 ▶ Planning Guide

191 ▶ Index

chapter one
PRINCIPLES

Whether you live in a small house or simply have some less-than-generous spaces in a large house, cramped quarters pose decorating challenges. In the pages that follow, you'll learn about principles that can help you overcome those challenges and make your rooms feel larger and function better.

A word about how to use this chapter: Each section explores one of six principles for dealing with small spaces. The text explains the principle, followed by bulleted ideas for ways to put it to work. Photos illustrate specific applications, but the bulleted ideas go further to give you even more options.

You may have heard the conventional wisdom that says when a room is small, you should paint the walls white or off-white to make the space seem larger. Or that it's best to pick only tiny fabric patterns, if you use pattern at all. Or that strong textures are best left out to avoid making the room appear too busy (and thus, even smaller). Not necessarily true!

All these points are sometimes valid, but there are many times when it's best to do just the opposite. Then you can make a deliberate decision to break the "rules" for small spaces and use deep-tone walls, an exuberant pattern, or a tapestry of textures.

Unconvinced? See how nature does it: Think of how dusk plays tricks with distance perception on a narrow road, or how the dark night sky recedes into infinity. Even small trees don't necessarily have tiny leaves. And when nature creates a sunlit opening in the forest, harmonious textures form masses of pattern as each variety of plant finds its ideal spot in the limited space. Timeless and always seeking balance, nature has a lot to teach the home decorator.

This book breaks down natural concepts into easy-to-remember principles that work in small spaces—to teach you how and when to break the old rules.

DEEP COLOR

Walls recede, especially at night, when painted a deep color. Before deciding on the final color, consider when you probably will be spending the most time in the room. If there's plenty of natural light, you can go with a darker color even for strictly "daytime" rooms.

▶ **Choose a darker value of a color used elsewhere in the room.** Draw the tone from a fabric, painting, or rug, picking a shade deep enough to act as a rich foil for lighter items. Flat nonreflective paint recedes more than that with sheen and also disguises blemishes on the walls better.

▶ **Accent with a lighter color woodwork—or not.** If the moldings have character, paint them in a contrasting light color. If they are not particularly appealing, then make them almost disappear by painting them in the semigloss version of the flat wall color.

▶ **Increase perceived space by using the same colors in adjoining rooms.** Creating a long line of sight so the eyes can see without interruption makes two small rooms look more like one large room.

▶ **Remove heavy window treatments to let in natural light** or use multiple sources of artificial light. Dark walls absorb far more light than paler ones, so good lighting is critical.

CREATE A SETTING Garnet red walls form a rich backdrop for antique furnishings in an adjoining living room and dining room. Crisp off-white woodwork adds architectural interest, but the walls, aside from adding color, seem to recede.

NO-COLOR COLOR

Using a neutral palette throughout is one of the best ways to push back the walls. The eye can freely roam through a neutral palette, whereas a bolder color could be a distracting element that would demand the eye's attention.

▶ **Accent with black, white, or wood-tone accessories.** Touches of these noncolors add the drama, freshness, and warmth that keep an all-neutral room from being boring.

▶ **Consolidate mismatched furniture with paint or slipcovers.** A hodgepodge of colors can be too distracting in a small space; unify with neutral slipcovers, upholstery, and painted or color-washed wooden pieces in a shade drawn from the wall color.

▶ **Take advantage of the soothing effects of neutrals.** These gentle colors got their name precisely because they are neutral. Neither too bold nor too retiring, they create a tranquil environment. Choose similar shades of taupe, pale gray, beige, tan, or cream for walls and furnishings.

▶ **Adapt the no-color color principle to use one main color, even one that's not a neutral, throughout the room.** The point is to avoid competing colors, saving them for small accents.

SIMPLE ELEGANCE *[left]* An absence of color puts the emphasis on comfort and conversation in this space-challenged living room.

CASUAL COVER-UP *[above right]* Unbleached canvas slipcovers hide mismatched or even somewhat damaged furniture.

WHITE ON LIGHT *[center right]* Pristine white against taupe is a sophisticated color scheme.

BRIGHT AND AIRY *[below right]* White linens, broad expanses of glass, and no-color accessories stretch space in a serene bedroom and sitting room combination.

NEUTRAL + ONE COLOR

Enliven a small space by sticking to white or a palette of neutral tones and adding one bold, attention-grabbing accent color to lead the eye where you want it to go. Use this color with restraint: Try it on one wall, a dominant piece of furniture, a large painting, a vase of flowers, a collection of accessories, or bright throw pillows.

▶ **Use the accent color as a bridge.** Repeat the accent color on walls in an adjoining room or in a fabric or a border. Continue to use it sparingly, but in a different way. (See lower photo on *page 65*.)

A FAVORITE PIECE *[above]* The dramatic Chinese cabinet finished in cinnabar lacquer provides a jolt of color in an otherwise subdued neutral dining room.

THE ART OF EMPHASIS *[right]* A poster with a black frame gains importance from the bright orange-red wall on which it hangs, becoming a vibrant focal point.

BRAULT
MERVEILLEUSEMENT GAZEUSE

DEEPER BACKGROUND
[opposite] Periwinkle blue walls
are the backdrop for coordinating
prints and liberal doses of white in
the bedroom, keeping it from
being too frilly.

JUST A HINT *[above right]* The
dining area is almost all white, but
small amounts of one color keep it
from appearing bland.

COLOR VARIATIONS *[below
right]* As long as they are close,
accent colors needn't match
exactly. Unobstructed windows
let ample light reflect from the
newly whitewashed walls.

LIGHT AND BRIGHT

White or very pale colors increase the
brightness of a room by reflecting light.
Sprinkling one or two accent colors throughout the
room is a variation on using neutrals plus one area of
bold color, as on *pages 12–13*.

▶ **Take advantage of all available light.** The primary
purpose of a window is to let in natural light, so keep
window treatments simple and avoid blocking the
light with heavy layers of drapery.

▶ **Choose fabrics with the same accent color but in
different patterns or textures.** Many manufacturers
offer complementary fabric patterns in the same
color. Take along fabric samples to be sure of a match
or complement when shopping for other furnishings.

CONNECT THE ROOMS [above]
A large toile pattern keeps the eye moving between the background and the design. The same pattern links the next room to this one.

BOLD, BUT BEARABLE [opposite]
Consider using a large pattern in a small area for drama. To allow one strong pattern to be the star, keep other colors to a minimum.

PATTERNS LARGE & SMALL

When using a bold pattern, keep other patterns to a minimum. Small spaces don't preclude the use of large patterns, but they do require that the pattern be used as a main element. If you've fallen in love with a pattern, go ahead and use it—but do be monogamous. Unless they share the same colors or have other similarities (as with the rug, *below right*), it's best to use only one pattern in a small room.

▶ **Repeat colors in the pattern with blocks of solid color or subdued patterns or stripes.** Large pieces of furniture, walls, rugs, and other elements look better when they complement, but don't compete with, the main pattern. Unify the room in as many ways as you can.

▶ **Draw the eye into adjoining rooms by repeating the pattern, but in smaller touches, for continuity.**
If you use a bold pattern as a main element in one room, use the same pattern on a pillow, a chair, or perhaps the trim on curtains in the next room.

▶ **Set up a dynamic of eye motion to add depth to small, boxy spaces.** Toile fabric in the rooms shown here creates a push-pull effect as the eye lands first on the pattern of the scene, then wanders into the white background, and then back to the pattern—over and over.

FIELDS OF FLOWERS A small pattern of delicate blossoms unifies a room that must serve as both a sitting and dining area. Draped from pegs on the walls, the fabric gains dimension that differentiates it from the smooth upholstery without adding another pattern element.

There's a difference between real space—which means having adequate room for activities and the items that go into a house—and apparent or visual space, which refers to the eye's perception that the space is large enough. This is because the scale of everything in a room is relative to everything else in that room. Areas that are too small gain more apparent space when you use furnishings in an appropriate scale, divide the room into zones for different activities, and arrange the furniture to create an easy flow of traffic between the zones.

What determines if the furniture scale is right for the room? And if you divide a room into areas, aren't you cutting a space that's already too small into even smaller parts?

Making such decisions is not so complicated once you learn a few pointers. In this section you'll see some good examples that will show you how to use the right furniture in the right arrangements.

PLAN THE ROUTE Clearly defined zones for dining and conversation create smaller, more intimate areas (even in large rooms). The open floor plan here seems larger than it is because the traffic patterns go between the zones rather than through them. Each seating area is further defined by area rugs and matching upholstery for chairs.

DIVIDE AND CONQUER

Arrange furniture in zones for particular
activities, such as dining, watching television,
or having a conversation. Dividing the space into
several small and intimate conversation zones is
usually preferable to having one large group of
chairs in which everyone seated is expected to talk
with everyone else.

▶ **Position furniture away from the walls.** The ideal
way to arrange furniture for the best zoning may
mean that sofas and tables don't necessarily line up
along the walls. Consider placing beds, sofas,
cabinets, and other large pieces of furniture at an
angle rather than parallel to walls.

▶ **Anchor a furniture grouping and delineate it from
others by creating an "island" with an area rug.**
A guideline for positioning furniture on the rug is
that all legs of a particular piece should either be
completely on the rug or completely off of it.

▶ **Leave unobstructed pathways between the zones**
for predictable traffic patterns across the room
or between different rooms. If possible, arrange
the furniture so that someone needn't cut directly
through a conversational area in order to walk across
the room.

UNCONVENTIONAL PLACEMENT

Reexamine your preconceived notions of how a room ought to look. There are times when placing the furniture at an angle, or shifting it toward the center of a room, results in a room that functions better and has a better traffic flow. The most interesting smaller homes are frequently those where creativity overcomes predictability.

▶ **A bed sometimes CAN be placed under a window.** Ideally every bedroom would have an unobstructed wall wide enough for a bed, no matter what size. If the only spot wide enough for a bed is directly under or beside a window, don't despair. Potential drafts were once the main reason for not sleeping there, but with today's tightly fitted and insulated windows, this is not usually a problem. Window treatments can also help block drafts.

▶ **Consider the corners.** Placing a large piece, such as a cabinet, an entertainment center, a bed, or a desk at an angle is an easy way to loosen up the arrangement and get away from the boxy look of many rooms. If the empty space behind it bothers you, then place a tall plant there. Or use the hidden space to store items you rarely need.

▶ **Display accessories with flair.** While every room needs a focal point that draws immediate attention, it's good to include minifocal points too. A handpainted piece of furniture, a unique vase holding flowers, interesting fabrics on pillows, or pictures hung in unusual spots serve the purpose of fooling the eye into focusing on something other than the size of the space.

FINDING AN ANGLE *[left]* With limited wall space, the large bed tucks into the corner. Avoiding bulky window treatments and using space under the bed and skirted table for storage also create more apparent space.

GOING WITH THE FLOW *[left]*
Guests can wander into the next room without interrupting the conversation in front of the fireplace. Angling the furniture makes the arrangement more intimate and less formal.

UNUSUAL ARRANGEMENT *[below]*
Slim legs on the desk at the foot of the bed create little visual weight and don't obstruct the view. Placing the desk here frees wall space elsewhere in the small bedroom for other uses.

▶ *INCLUDE AT LEAST ONE TALL ELEMENT—a bookcase or an armoire, for instance—in every room. Create interest at floor level, too, with a patterned rug or a basket of pinecones beneath a table. The idea is to keep the eye moving to distract it from the actual size of the room.*

LARGE & SMALL

Pay attention to the visual weight of furniture, not just its actual size. Pale-color furniture or pieces with legs appear lighter than boxy, dark, or upholstered pieces—try to achieve a balance. Lessen the perceived weight of heavy upholstered pieces by slipcovering them in a pale fabric. Or choose a table with a glass top to fool the eye into thinking it's not there and thereby increase the apparent space in the room.

▶ **Choose furniture in a scale appropriate for its use and also for the people who will use it.** A large man won't enjoy having to perch on a dainty chair much too small for him. On the other hand, massively clunky armchairs may be sturdy enough for children but will overwhelm a small room. Aim for a balance with well-designed furniture in the right scale to complement the room, your family, and your lifestyle.

▶ **Observe the adage "Less is more."** If you like large furniture, use fewer, more versatile pieces rather than cramming too much into the room. (See the photo on *pages 6–7*.)

OUT OF THE WAY *[above left]* A pair of stools and a compact table provide dining space in a nook less than 3 feet deep.

STORY TIME *[left]* This comfortable reading chair is large enough for two, yet its pastel color keeps it from seeming overly heavy.

EAT AND RUN *[right]* Metal bar stools fit under the table when the family isn't eating breakfast.

TABLE FOR TWO *[opposite]* A petite round table is large enough for dining or reading the paper.

DRAW THE EYE UPWARD [*above*]
Almost any room, no matter how small, offers opportunities to draw attention to something above eye level. In the tiny pass-through between the kitchen and the dining room, ceiling-height glass-front cabinets and pictures above the door add interest and lessen the sense of confinement.

HIGH & LOW

The space in an area always includes more than floor space. It also means cubic space and all those horizontal and vertical extensions of sight into adjoining areas that increase the apparent size. By drawing the eye to space above and below eye level where it's unencumbered by furniture, and increasing the field of vision beyond the usual reference points, you can fool the brain into perceiving that any space is larger than it really is.

▶ **Accent the vertical.** Floor-to-ceiling columns and ceiling-height cabinets and bookcases all lift the eye, as do attractive crown moldings, decorative curtain rods, ceiling fans, and similar elements. Accent a doorway by hanging paintings, a mirror, or a carving above it. Be wary of using deep wallpaper borders with 8-foot ceilings—they lead the eye downward.

▶ **Lead the eye with art.** Conventional wisdom says that you hang a painting with its center at eye level, which is fine unless you're trying to make a room seem taller. Then it can be helpful to "stack" the display by hanging two or three pictures or other artful items in a vertical column.

▶ **Maximize the perceived height of the room.** To avoid feeling too enclosed, paint low ceilings a light color. High or vaulted ceilings draw the eye upward even more if they are an accent color or textured.

▶ **Draw attention to open areas of the floor.** Add interest with an area rug, textured flooring, or a rich color that attracts the eye.

A LONG WAY FROM THE TOP
[opposite below] When guests sit
on low chairs or pillows, the rest
of the room seems taller and more
spacious by comparison, even if
ceilings are only standard height.
Floor-to-ceiling shelves take full
advantage of vertical space too.

UPLIFTING ELEMENTS *[above]*
Hanging one picture above another
creates a strategy for leading
the eye toward the top of the
room. Other elements of interest
near the ceiling—a fan, crown
molding, and decorative curtain
medallions—do the same.

Clutter: The very word inspires visions of messy closets and unfathomable kitchen drawers. No one starts out wanting it, but over the years, almost everyone accumulates clutter in the dark recesses of the home. Eventually it spills out where it doesn't belong, which is easy in a small house where every inch of space is precious. So how can you tame the clutter before it drives you to distraction?

You'll begin to make progress when you start looking at your entire home—not just those areas set aside for storage—as a box filled with space. Consider every cubic foot in every room as a potential storage area, including the space close to walls, around windows and doors, above eye level, beneath stairways, and under furniture.

You may be surprised to find that you've been shortchanging yourself by not making your existing space work as hard as it can to help resolve your clutter problems. But there's no time like the present to change the situation.

WRAPAROUND STORAGE

Leverage your space. In one sense, to leverage means to use something you already have to make more of something you need. For instance, if you have only a certain number of square feet, you'll gain far more storage with shelves that go to the top of the room than you would with a piece of furniture in the same spot. Consider these ideas for using previously wasted floor space at the edges of a room:

▶ **Surround a window or door with shelving.** Run the shelving from wall to wall or use purchased units such as bookcases or cabinets to simulate built-ins. Join the two sides with a continuous shelf across the top or with a piece of crown molding matching that used elsewhere in the room.

▶ **Leave an opening to display art if you fill an entire wall with shelving.** Paint that wall an accent color before installing the shelves to create a focal point where there is none or to add depth to a boxy room.

▶ **Plan extra-deep shelves at the base of the unit.** Top the deeper shelves with a finished surface (useful for serving or as a work surface) before continuing with shelves to the ceiling.

▶ **Add doors at the base** (and maybe the top) of built-in shelving to conceal extra-large or unsightly items or electronic equipment.

OVER THE TOP Surrounding this French door with built-ins creates shelving that totals more than six times the actual floor space used, without interfering with traffic flow. A handy work surface caps deep shelves at the base, and the top shelf extends in an unbroken line over the door to join the two sides together visually.

STRAIGHT & NARROW

Add shallow shelves for storage. Nearly every home has numerous spots where 3- or 4-inch-deep shelving will fit, even if it's only between vertical studs in the wall. Unless it's an outside wall or above an electrical outlet, consider breaking through and claiming the unused space.

▶ **Install adjustable shelves in any storage cabinet.** You may want to store different items in the future, and readjusting shelves will allow taller items to fit.

▶ **Line the back of a shallow cabinet with a mirror.** It will reflect the room in front of it, increasing the perceived size of the space enormously.

▶ **Line a hallway with shallow recessed cabinets to display collectibles or store glassware.** Add glass shelves and lights at the top for display or add cabinet doors to hide stored items. Because most wall studs are 16 inches apart, the shelves can be up to 15 inches wide and 3 inches deep without taking up any floor space.

▶ **Add doors that match the walls to disguise cabinets between the studs.** Or panel both the walls and the doors; then add invisible hinges for an almost seamless surface (see *left* photo on *page 34*).

▶ **Hide shallow storage for valuables behind a mirror or painting.** No one except you will know it's there.

RECESS TIME *[opposite]* Tucked between wall studs, glass shelves display an attractive collection of pottery. Rounded shelves mounted on the upper cabinets are ideal for favorite items, pretty flowers, or sun-loving plants.

TALL ORDER *[right]* Formerly wasted space between a pair of arched windows holds a tall but shallow cabinet fitted with decorative glass doors. It takes up little counter space.

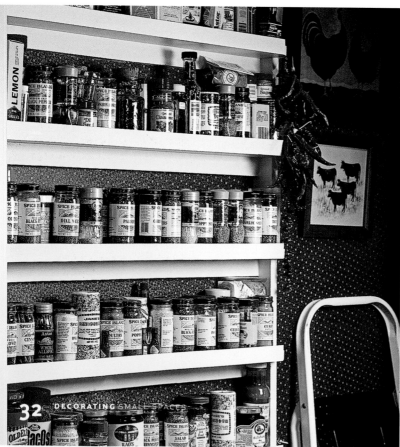

SMALL CHANGES

Look for places to add extra kitchen storage. *Clockwise, from opposite top left:*

HANDY ACCESS Remove the doors on a cabinet and use sturdy pull-out willow baskets to hold napkins, towels, and placemats.

TURNAROUND SPACE Rather than coping with too-deep shelves, line a closet with shallow shelves on two or three sides for use as a pantry.

APPLIANCE GARAGE Store blenders, food processors, and mixers conveniently on the counter—they'll be out of sight behind a pull-down tambour door.

COLLECTOR'S DELIGHT Take up minimal wall space with a wooden plate rack to display some of your prettiest dishes.

END OF THE LINE Put wasted space at the end of a counter to good use by mounting a storage unit on the wall.

STAIRWAY STORAGE Install shelves in the space beneath the stairs, making them shallow at the top and deep enough near the floor to store wine bottles.

ALPHABETICAL ORDER Arrange spices on shelving deep enough for only one bottle; they will be easy to find when needed.

CABINET CAPABILITIES

Add a cabinet to expand your storage. Spacious, ready-made cabinets come in many sizes, styles, and finishes and are too useful to be relegated only to kitchens and baths. Imagine roomy cabinets in other locations. To give basic units a custom appearance, paint them to match the other woodwork in the room.

▶ **Build a storage wall at one end of a room by combining various cabinets and shelves to fill the space.** Even though it takes up little actual floor space, such a wall unit will organize and store an amazing amount in a child's or teen's room.

▶ **Add a rod inside a stock pantry or broom-closet cabinet to create a closet in an office that doubles as a guest room.** It looks fine as part of a bookcase unit and provides much-needed hanging space.

▶ **Stack slender cabinets to fill in a narrow space between two doors or windows.** Remove the doors and put a mirror in the back or replace door panels with mirrors to create the effect of another window.

SPACE-SAVVY SYSTEM [above]
A file drawer in the cabinet keeps household papers and important documents in one convenient place. Shallow storage along the hallway is almost invisible when the panelled doors are closed.

BENEATH THE WINDOWS [right]
Flank the fireplace with made-to-fit base cabinets to keep magazines, hobby equipment, or games handy but out of sight.

STORAGE SEATING [opposite]
Standard kitchen cabinets can be the base for an entry-hall bench—the storage beneath it is a convenient bonus for storing rain shoes and boots. Drill holes in the bench bottom for ventilation.

SQUEEZE OUT EXTRA STORAGE

Check out your house from top to bottom to find unused cubic feet of space even if you think you've exhausted every possibility for storing those items you can't live without. You may see where you can incorporate ideas similar to these:

▶ **Add a shallow shelf around the perimeter of the room, a foot or so below the ceiling.** Use it to display plates or other collectibles you want to keep away from little hands.

▶ **Place the bed on a platform with pull-out drawers for shoes, purses, or out-of-season clothing.** Use underbed storage boxes if you have a standard bed frame. For a child's room, choose a bunk bed unit with storage underneath.

▶ **Line a pass-through between rooms with shallow cabinets on each side.** Glass doors take up less visual space than those made of solid wood and come in transparent and translucent patterns. In extra-small areas leave off the doors and put a mirror in the back.

▶ **Attach wooden spice racks to the back of a door.** Store unbreakable items such as socks or toiletries in plastic containers in these shallow racks.

POTTING ROOM *[opposite]* An impossibly narrow room contains a whole wall of cabinets, but see-through doors keep it from seeming too claustrophobic.

CLEAN EXIT *[below left]* Storage next to the garage door holds boots, hats, gloves, and sports equipment for quick access as the family comes and goes.

WINE STORAGE *[below]* Dividers in an above-eye-level wine rack form an attractive grid above a mirrored bar that expands the view. A glass shelf stores crystal.

If you could wave a magic wand, your present house would be the perfect size for your family, it would look beautiful, and the space would adapt to fit as your lifestyle changes. Instead you may find that your space is cramped, it doesn't fit your furniture, and it's not quite the house of your dreams. But like a magician whose sleight of hand changes your perception, you can often fool the eye into thinking that your space is larger, no matter what its actual size. The trick is to do it with knowledge, finesse, and great style.

Begin with the simple part: A room is basically a big box of space surrounded by walls, a floor, and a ceiling—six boundaries. There's at least one door and usually the exterior wall has windows—these provide relief from the boxiness by expanding your line of sight to include areas outside the actual room. Too often these openings just don't do an adequate job. The room still feels uncomfortably small—and its dimensions aren't going to change.

If you find yourself in this situation, it's time to pull out a space-expanding trick or two and transform the room. This chapter will let you in on the secrets of decorating with illusion.

SPACE EXPANDERS

Use more mirrors. Glass mirrors, when first used, were very expensive. Today they are recognized as the incredible bargains they are because reflected space is more effective than anything else at liberating rooms from feeling too confined.

Use mirrors generously—floor to ceiling, on walls, above wainscoting, under cabinets, inside cupboards, between windows, in a niche, or in dark corners—to introduce a sleek, contemporary accent and, best of all, to add the illusion of spaciousness.

The gleaming glass surface reflects items in the room and also amplifies light from every source. A wall-to-wall mirror can actually double the visual space in a room, and if a smaller mirror is hung directly opposite, the views stretch out to infinity.

▶ **Hang a mirror in a windowless bathroom or hallway.** It will open up the room almost as much as a window. If a mirror in any room can reflect an actual window, it will look like its twin.

▶ **Extend the field of vision with a mirror "transom" over the door.** Hang a horizontal mirror—it will reflect only the upper part of the room and almost appear to be clear glass.

TWICE THE ROOM *[right]* The oversize framed mirror leaning against the wall (but safely secured at the top) effectively doubles the amount of perceived space in this neutral-tone bedroom.

REFLECTING ON LIFE *[right]*
One large framed mirror doubles the impact of the fern green color in this bedroom. The reading chair in front of the mirror gains the benefit of reflected ambient light, which supplements light from the floor lamp.

CRYSTAL ILLUSION *[opposite above]* Adding mirror and glass doors to a small freehanging cabinet changes it from a dark storage area to a vibrant, light-reflective element in the room.

VANISHING WALL *[opposite below]* Three generous panels of mirror look like openings between rooms, yet they're only reflecting the windows and ceiling of the room with the bar. Leaving the center free of shelves intensifies the illusion of openness.

LIGHT REFLECTORS

The more light inside a house, the roomier it usually appears. Take advantage of the light-reflecting quality of mirrors by using them in novel ways to add life to dark areas. Sometimes it's not an actual lack of space that makes a room seem small. It may simply feel constricted because it has too many dark corners.

▶ **Install a mirror above a bar counter or under kitchen cabinets.** Doing this will make it seem as though there's an opening into the next room, expanding the eye's line of sight.

▶ **Line a cabinet with a mirror to display crystal.** The facets on crystal pick up silvery reflections from the mirror, then the mirror bounces them back so that part of the room dances with light.

▶ **Use glass shelves in front of mirrors to minimize distracting elements and add a clean-lined accent.** Remember that a glass shelf needs plenty of support to hold heavy objects. Short spans of shelving are better than one extremely long shelf.

▶ **Bring the outdoors into a room with too few windows by creating an indoor greenhouse.** Line a cabinet with a mirrored back and add glass shelves at least a foot apart. Place grow lights in the top and periodically rotate the plants to different shelves to expose them all to adequate light.

MULTIPLE SOURCES Lights in the ceiling and under the top cabinets provide excellent task lighting in this kitchen (which appears larger than it really is because it was photographed with a wide-angle lens). Even more dramatic light comes through the translucent door and from inside the gridded cabinet.

THE LIGHT FANTASTIC

Good lighting is critically important when space is tight. Some of the discomforting feeling of being too cramped, in fact, can be alleviated by making the space you already have function as well as possible. This requires making sure that each room has three types of lighting: ambient lighting (for overall illumination), task lighting (to supply light for activities), and accent lighting (to add the extra sparkle that keeps a room on its toes). Many small spaces also tend to be dark spaces, and plenty of light can fool the eye into thinking they are larger.

▶ **Plan multiple sources of lighting in every room.** One single light in the ceiling is hardly ever the way to go. Shadowy corners seem to close in and make the room appear smaller. Ideally the light should come from several different heights and directions.

▶ **Switch from a wooden door to a glass door.** If privacy is a factor, choose translucent glass, which will let in natural light even if it doesn't offer a clear view. Glass works as a space-expander in either exterior or interior doors (see *pages 14* and *53*).

CLEAN AND SIMPLE [above]
Sleek shuttered windows complement the tailored furniture. A horizontal board supported by vertical members adds interest to the basically plain window wall. A translucent divider with one sliding panel allows the adjoining room to share the light.

BUMPED OUT [opposite left]
Expand the view with a sunny indoor greenhouse by installing a bay or boxed bay window in place of the existing window. In a small room it can make an amazing difference that goes far beyond its actual size and it's also an ideal showcase for plants.

GRACEFUL WISP [opposite right]
Soften the severely rectangular lines of the window frame in an already boxy room with a swoop of diaphanous fabric and leave the rest of the window bare. For privacy add either blinds or a pull-down shade behind the valance, lowering it only when needed.

OPEN IT UP

Simplify the window treatments. Elaborate treatments have no place in an area that's already feeling too cramped. The best approach is to handle the need for privacy and light control by using shades, blinds, shutters, or sheer curtains on rods. If your privacy situation allows, use only a decorative valance at the top or even nothing at all. Windows are the eyes of a house—keep them open.

▶ **Accent the vertical.** Install curtain rods near the top of the room rather than on the window frame. This draws attention toward the ceiling, especially if you use decorative finials on the rods. (Buy longer curtains if you do this.) Unless your ceilings are high, avoid complicated or heavy-fabric valances laden with trim—they make ceilings appear lower.

GENTLE SUBTERFUGE

Resort to camouflage. To many people the word camouflage brings to mind only a jumble of green, brown, and beige spots, or the woods. If space feels cramped or you realize you'll need to put off buying new furniture until later, then how could camouflage help?

Tricks of concealment or hiding (which is all camouflage really means) can cover up unsightly furnishings and also do a lot to make your space seem larger. The ideas on these pages—and others in the book—will help you put this principle to work.

▶ **Decide what you don't like and figure out ways to hide it.** Now that you've seen how color affects the perception of space, your furniture may not be what you want. Try painting too-dark wooden pieces in a neutral shade or using one fabric to slipcover several pieces of furniture whose colors clash.

▶ **Switch from a wooden table to one with a glass top.** There's no better way to open up the center of a room or to reveal the pattern in a pretty rug. You may not even need to buy a new table; often an old base looks fine under a new glass top. Anything that is stable and will support the weight of the glass will work as a base.

SEE YOU LATER, RADIATOR *[above right]* Offering reliable heat but little in the way of beauty, a radiator gains new glamour with a cover that functions as an extra serving table.

FIND THE FURNITURE *[center right]* Neutral slipcovers and upholstery blend a whole roomful of jarringly mismatched furniture into one harmonious grouping— this makes the living room space seem larger.

UNDERCOVER OFFICE *[below right]* In this room tucked into formerly unused attic space, tailored slipcovers hide things best left unseen, including unattractive file cabinets and ugly tables.

THE DISAPPEARING TABLE *[opposite]* Despite its ample size, this glass-top table takes up little or no visual space and items on its surface almost seem to float. Glass tables come in a variety of shapes too.

THE BIG SCREEN

Hide the television. When you like having the television where it's convenient to watch, but don't like the way its blank screen takes over the room, resort to some simple trickery and hide it. Aside from keeping your television in an entertainment center made for the purpose, there are several other options:

▶ **Place the television on a shelf inside a spacious armoire** or a cabinet with doors that close. If the television is too deep for the space, try removing the back or a portion of the back just large enough to accommodate the excess. Newer televisions often have flat screens that don't require much depth; simply drill a hole large enough for the plug.

▶ **Tuck the television into unused space** beneath the stairs, facing it toward the room. Cover the opening with doors made to fit.

▶ **Position the television on a short, sturdy table with casters.** Roll it into a nearby closet whenever you aren't watching it.

▶ **Install sliding paper panels (called shoji screens) or draperies** on ceiling-height rods in front of large-screen televisions and close them when the set is not in use. This increases the drama of a home theater.

PLAYING DRESS-UP *[opposite]*
Few people would guess that behind this handsome mirror there's a secret. The oversize mirror looks as though it's hanging on the fireplace wall, where it greatly expands the room's apparent size.

SECRET REVEALED *[left]*
Mounted on heavy-duty tracks at the top and bottom, the mirror slides to the side easily with just the touch of a hand, and the television is ready for viewing. The television sits on a deep shelf to one side of the insulated chimney pipe rising from the fireplace.

BACK-TO-BACK STORAGE
[opposite and below] There was only one way to add a closet to the adjoining room and it required borrowing space from this sitting room. Increasing the depth of the closet added space for a television on the sitting-room side.

Picture-frame molding surrounds the opening and a handpainted window shade pulls down from behind it to become "art" when the television is not in use. The antique mantel displays favorite treasures, but the fireplace itself is not functional.

INVITING VIEW

Lead the eye where you want it to go. The human eye is enthusiastic and adventurous—it is quite naturally drawn to whatever is new or seems to offer the promise of excitement. Small spaces tend to bore it, so in order to create more interest, the home decorator must offer help by deliberately leading the eye beyond the actual boundaries of the room. This can be done with good planning or some simple changes.

▶ **Line up openings in a symmetrical manner.** Openings that progress from one room to the next are more attractive if there's a strong focal point at the end.

▶ **Enlarge standard doorways or cased openings by making them wider or extending the opening up to the ceiling.** If support is a problem, consider using a ceiling-height column at each side of the opening.

▶ **Avoid putting roadblocks in the line of sight.** Encountering a tall, bulky piece of furniture, such as a chest of drawers, at eye level just as you walk into a narrow space makes the room seem smaller.

NONSTOP VIEW *[opposite]* The unusual floor plan in this house creates few barriers for the eye, which can roam freely between rooms, thanks to glass shelves and doors. An added advantage of having glass form a large part of the walls is that natural light floods even interior areas.

READY FOR COMPANY *[above]* A small kitchen feels more open and hospitable because it has a view of the adjoining living room and hallway. The window pass-through is a fairly standard vision expanding device, but the other wall has interesting narrow openings to display pottery.

DISTANT VIEWS [*opposite* and *below*] Both of these rooms are excellent examples of how looking beyond one room into others makes a space seem less hemmed in by walls and more inviting to the eye. Widen any openings, align the doors, or use glass-paned French doors between the rooms for maximum effect.

THE WAY TO GO *[right]* There's always a view up ahead on this stair landing that visually expands the actual boundaries of the room. A pot of real flowering branches sits on the floor to heighten the painted illusion.

ANOTHER VIEW *[opposite below left]* Hand-painted tiles behind the desk almost fool the eye into thinking they are real. The painted landing wall to the right of the desk creates the impression that the room is much larger than it is.

SUNNY DAY *[opposite above]* Being stuck doing the laundry in a confining space seems far more pleasant when that room has blue skies and gentle breezes.

ROOM WITH A VIEW *[opposite below right]* This room-expanding view of the mountains is nothing more than a painted niche in a narrow hallway, yet it transforms the closed-in effect that the formerly blank wall once had.

ELABORATE RUSE

Fake the view. Harness the power of painted illusion and you can be in a cramped apartment or a room with tiny windows, yet still enjoy a glorious view of the Italian countryside, the mountains of Switzerland, the coast of sunny California—or possibly all three.

The technique of painting something in a manner that could conceivably trick someone into believing it's the real thing is called *trompe l'oeil*, which is French for "fool the eye." It requires artistic talent and a good command of perspective, but the space-enhancing possibilities are endless.

Just in case you were born without the genes of an artist or can't find an artist who specializes in such work, there are other ways to exchange your closed-in quarters for a room with a view:

▶ **Many home improvement stores sell individual trompe l'oeil panels to paste directly on the wall.** Shuttered windows, teapot-filled cupboards, or arches—they come in many different designs and you can trim them to fit your particular location.

▶ **Check wallpaper stores for scenic papers.** Some papers are vertical repeats of a painted scene, but others are actual photographs of the outdoors.

▶ **Consider stenciling a "view."** Stencils have changed in the last few years, and you can now order kits with multiple stencils to create all kinds of scenes. Look for stencil companies in home furnishings magazines or on the Internet.

You've heard that old expression "It's not written in stone," but you may not have applied it to your space problems. Consider this: A baby has a crib and changing table—yet that same child as a teen would prefer stereo equipment and a computer desk. The bedroom is the same, but use of the space is entirely different.

Families and needs often change, even if your space doesn't. One day it simply makes more sense to convert the guest room to an exercise room. Or to make one room do the work of two and add bookshelves to the dining room so you can use it as a library. One piece of furniture can also do the work of two, which is a big plus when floor space is at a premium. An open-up ottoman, for instance, can be a footrest, extra storage, or a serving table for coffee.

It's a radical change to rethink the way you use space in your house, but the actual conversion can often be easy. In this section you'll see ideas that may inspire you to convert your space to something that suits you better. And if you decide to change it again later—well, it's not written in stone.

PORTABLE CLOSET SPACE

Add another closet. It's hard to realize that people once lived with no closets at all. Today the almost universal complaint about houses, small or large, is that they don't have enough storage.

It's a truism that no matter how many closets you may have, they will all be full. But what can you do when it seems there's no possible place to build another closet?

▶ **Make a bathroom closet.** If you need storage for out-of-season clothes more than you need that extra bathtub, set up a hanging rack there instead. Hide it with a pretty, opaque shower curtain.

▶ **Hang draperies from a rod on the ceiling and use them as "closet doors."** If you have even 18 inches to spare at the end of a room, there's enough room for a closet. Outfit the space with some of the many closet organizers available.

▶ **Slipcover a shelving unit to make a freestanding storage closet.** Stack the shelves with boxes covered with matching fabric for a coordinated appearance.

OUT OF SIGHT Tailored draperies are a high-style coverup for a closet that is only needed temporarily. The rod attaches to the ceiling with hardware that is easily removed, and all of the other closet accessories are freestanding.

DOUBLE-DUTY ROOMS

Change the way you use your rooms. In many homes, existing space is underutilized. If you have a room that's occupied for only a short time each day, then you may be able to get far more use from it than you are getting now. Luckily it's not often that a room is suited for only one use.

▶ **Make a partition between parts of the room with sliding curtains.** Close off more active (meaning messy) areas from quieter areas. Use curtains to separate the crafts area from the office, the laundry from the playroom, the sewing nook from the bedroom, or even to keep the kids from squabbling over territory. The partitioned room shown on these pages was originally a garage.

▶ **Add floor-to-ceiling shelves in the dining room, hallway, or stair landing.** These underused spaces are ideal for shallow bookshelves. Install track lighting for easy identification of titles. Create a lighter look by combining art, accessories, or even plants with the books on some of the shelves.

▶ **Turn the stairway into an art gallery.** For a changing display save a space on the landing where the main piece of art changes each season.

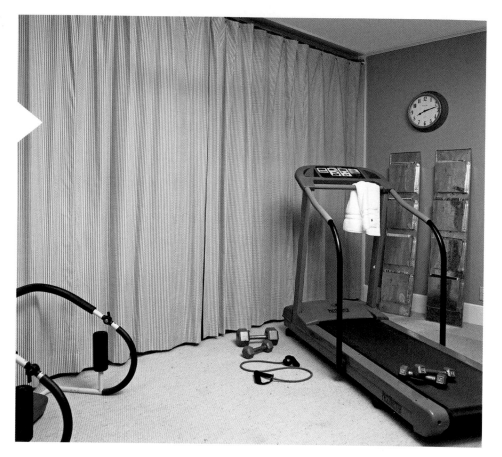

LAUNDRY UPGRADE *[above and opposite]* Waiting 30 minutes for the spin cycle to end seems easier when the time can be spent on exercise equipment just a few steps away. When the laundry is done, just close the curtains.

Behind the curtain there's a television and plenty of storage to help the laundry function better. Hanging racks, shelves with removable bins, a large can for detergent, and clothes baskets keep everything close at hand.

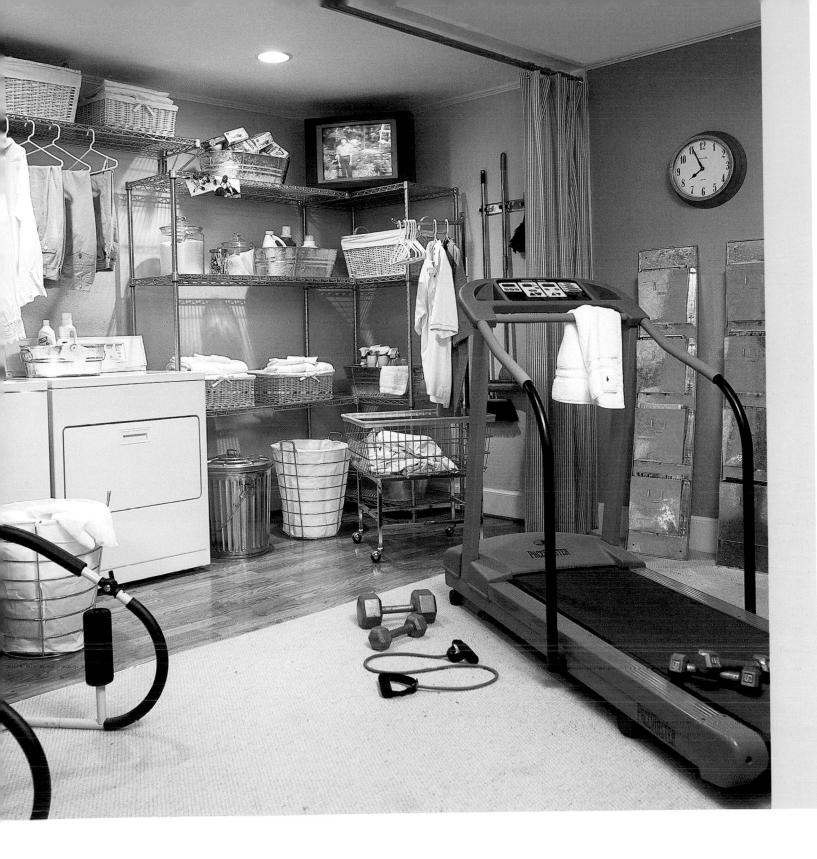

FOOD FOR THOUGHT Shelving takes up only a foot of width on each side of this dining room, yet it consolidates books once strewn all over the house. Reading or doing homework at the table is a given—and now reference books are close at hand.

ONE-ROOM WONDER This small space can serve as living room, dining room, gallery, extra bedroom, and library with a wall of interlocking cubes for storage.

BOOK NOOK *[right]* Are you mad for big, beautiful coffee table books, but find that they're too large for most bookcases? Then choose a table with a lower shelf and you'll have a perfect spot for all your favorite oversize books.

THE YOUNG CROWD *[opposite above]* It's a rare house that has enough room around the table when family and friends come over—all at one time. Stools slide under the table and out of the way unless they're providing extra seating for four youngsters.

COFFEE AND COMFORT *[opposite below]* An oversize ottoman is about as versatile as a piece of furniture can get. After serving as a table, it easily switches to a footrest or becomes the favorite spot for a youngster's naptime. Some ottomans open for extra storage space, which is handy for blankets and other bulky items.

DUAL-DESIGN FURNITURE

Choose furniture that serves more than one purpose. Innovative home furnishing designers have thought of a thousand ways to adapt furniture to small homes and smaller apartments—pieces open up, fold flat, push under, or even roll away.

▶ **Look for pieces to put to alternate uses.** A painted stepladder in front of a sunny window is a stunning display stand for plants, and they'll then take up more vertical space than floor space.

▶ **Put locking casters on furniture, especially tables or heavy pieces.** When having a party roll the table to the side of the room and use it for food display.

▶ **Cover round tables with floor-length cloths and use the space inside for extra storage.** Hide boxes or a storage-drawer unit under the cloth.

ARTISTIC LICENSE

Set aside space for doing what you love to do. You deserve a room that inspires your mind to roam—where ideas and art come together to create something of value. Having a room dedicated to painting, hobbies, or crafts may seem like an unattainable luxury in a house that's already straining at the seams, but with these ideas, gaining the space is definitely in the picture.

▶ **Dedicate a closet to storing crafts supplies.** Include space for an easel, a card table with folding legs, or a table on locking casters. Set up the easel or table in the room when you're working and put it back in the closet when you're finished.

▶ **Store supplies inside cabinets above the washer and dryer.** Staple plastic sheeting around ¼-inch-thick squares of plywood to make wipe-clean work surfaces (keep them between the appliances when not in use). Add a comfortable barstool and the room used only a few times a week for laundry becomes an ideal place for crafts or other projects.

HOME SCHOOLING [*opposite above*] Writing on the walls is encouraged in this room, where chalkboard paint, available at any hardware store, creates an ideal surface. A bank of stock cabinets with wall-mounted shelving above has two niches for desks that also come in handy for other sit-down activities, such as making crafts.

ARTISTS IN TRAINING [*opposite below*] Painting plain walls with chalkboard paint transforms the playroom into a creative incubator for young Picassos who can practice their art whenever they like. The dark walls wash clean easily, and the color, surprisingly, seems to increase the apparent space in the room.

NORTH LIGHT [*above*] Capturing the ideal light may seem easier than finding the extra space for a studio. If you can give up half of the garage, you can also create a studio by laying flooring and substituting French doors for the overhead door. Add both lighting and a translucent skylight for a reliably bright interior.

Squeezing out every possible inch of usable space is an art that can be learned, and once you learn it, you'll never look at a house in the same way. For instance if you're resigned to a typical builder house—average storage in an average number of average, boxy rooms—and you've done what you can to increase its livability, it's time to look again.

With overlooked space tucked under eaves and stairways, behind doors, and above and below eye level, most dwellings have at least a few areas that could be used more wisely. As you look, consider how much space you really need for specific uses. With good planning, it may be less than you think. By making a few changes to better use your own forgotten corners, you'll add to the space your family can use and have a more interesting, less average home too.

EXTRA CAPACITY *[right]* This large kitchen offers an idea that can easily be adapted to a smaller one: Along the back of the island, shelves behind transparent doors provide dust-free storage for accessories and multiple sets of china and crystal.

KITCHEN CROSSROAD

Use your island for storage. Traffic in a kitchen often revolves around a central island. This vital part of the busiest room may contain the cooktop or the sink, or it may be where you prepare food. But if it isn't helping you solve your storage problems too, it's a roadblock to progress. Consider the suggestions below and the functional island *[left]* to see how you can make your own private island absolutely indispensable for storage. Turn to *pages 102–103* to see even more hardworking island ideas.

▶ **Create back-up storage behind the island.** Increase the depth of the island by as little as 6 inches, then add shelves to the back. Doors keep the dust at bay.

▶ **If your island is large enough, use one end as the base for open glass shelves extending to the ceiling.** Supports hold the glass shelves steady, but the shelves take up a minimum of visual space while providing space for essentials.

▶ **Purchase a stainless-steel or wooden cart on casters to use as an island.** Many kitchen carts have drawers or shelves beneath the work surface, and some have a knife rack or pull-out cutting board at the side. Plus you can roll the cart out of the way.

IMPORTANT CHANGE

Convert underused space to an extra bath. No matter what size your family is, it's always nice to have an extra bath. Whether you're changing a closet into a powder room for guests or figuring out a way for a teenager to have her own shower, there may be a way to do it in less space than you think you need. The ideas shown here prove that where there's a will to make space, there's a way.

▶ **If the space won't accommodate the depth of built-in vanity cabinets, use a narrow countertop and shelves instead.** Store necessary items in slide-out baskets on the shelves.

▶ **Look into using a smaller-than-usual lavatory; there is a size for almost every situation, including corner installations.** Although home improvement stores usually stock only standard sizes, most of them will order special sizes.

▶ **Gain extra wall space by installing towel racks on the back of a door.** Be sure to use a doorstop that is deeper than the racks to keep them from hitting the wall when someone opens the door.

▶ **Use the space between studs for built-in cabinets.** This is especially handy for storing toiletries in slender bottles. Leave off the door and use shallow glass shelves and a mirrored back to visually expand the bathroom even more.

▶ **Double the apparent width in a bathroom with a wall-to-wall mirror.** This can keep a narrow room from seeming closed in.

SLIM OPPORTUNITY *[opposite, above* and *below]* A slim but deep former closet is large enough to turn into a guest bath. The key is the custom-made vanity, a slender curve of counter space that widens only to hold the sink and provide storage.

SLIVER OF SPACE *[left]* A thick slab of glass narrows dramatically to allow access through the bath doorway. Other space-expanding features are the pull-out towel bars and a wall-to-wall mirror.

UNDER THE EAVES *[below, left and right]* A sloping ceiling and dormer windows don't preclude having a spacious bath in the attic. The full-size tub has plenty of headroom under the shower, which has one fixed pane and a standard glass door instead of a shower curtain. The triangular dormer window opens from the top to admit fresh air while furnishing natural light. There's no place for a large mirror, but a smaller, easy-to-adjust mirror attaches at the bottom.

STAIRSTEP STORAGE

Put your staircase to work. The stairwell is a dominant element in any home that has one—in essence, it's a vertical well of mostly empty space above and below the steps. Typical stair railings are made of identical spindles that stand in a row like silent sentinels, offering safety against falls but nothing in the way of storage. Space below the staircase is often underused too, becoming a dark catchall or a too-deep closet with too little space for hanging clothes.

Although its broad walls are a good place to display paintings, the staircase in a space-deprived home should also work to create storage for essentials whenever possible.

▶ **Tuck an upright piano into the recess beneath the stairs.** The niche seems almost custom made for a special music area, so highlight the difference by accenting it with a different shade or a faux finish.
▶ **Fill the under-stairs area with a row of stock base cabinets for storage.** The top won't match the slope of the stairway, but so what? Add a marble slab or another surface and it will be a built-in server.

CHILDHOOD ESSENTIALS *[above left]* Deep storage cubes at the head of the stairs hold toys and sports paraphernalia for the upstairs occupants (and would also adapt well to a display of artwork). A broad shelf above the cubes makes a handy table.

LONG, LEAN BOOKCASE *[center left]* An oversize window behind the staircase opens up the view, but necessitates leaving the area beneath the steps open. The bookcase makes excellent use of the space, and its top shelf, directly beneath the sunny window, is ideal for plants.

STOP ALONG THE WAY *[below left]* A comfortable bench with an intriguing curved back takes the place of a stair railing. Deep, pull-out storage drawers form the base, and the cushioned top is a handy spot to place items before taking them upstairs.

CABINET EXTENSION *[opposite]* With cabinets extending into space reserved for a railing, this kitchen gained an enormous amount of "wall space" and storage. The smooth, sloping top of the cabinet repeats the angle of the railing and permits a good view of the upper steps.

OPEN TO IDEAS

Let the window do more than offer a view. An unadorned window might still be a feature you can show off. By opening up the room to the world outside, windows fulfill their main function, but some of them do even more. Stylish windows easily become main focal points in rooms, while the surrounding shelves add essential storage or display space too.

- ▶ **Extend the depth of an above-the-sink windowsill by adding a shallow shelf on brackets.** Flowering houseplants thrive in the almost constant light.

- ▶ **Install glass shelves in front of a window, lining up each shelf with a muntin (the strip separating the panes of glass).** Use shelves to showcase glass or other items that look best with light coming from behind them (see photo *opposite*).

- ▶ **Bump out the exterior window about 1 foot to create a ledge for plants.** Instead of installing a box bay (see photo *above right*), reinstall the existing window in the bumped-out wall and then panel the two sides with mirrors to reflect and add depth to the room. Tile the bottom to create a waterproof surface for the plants.

WELL-LIT STAGE *[left]* Sunlight is the most effective spotlight, especially when the object of attention is a collection of transparent glass. Notice that the shelves line up with window muntins for minimal distraction.

WINDOW BOX *[opposite above]* Almost every kitchen activity seems to involve the sink. A box bay window allows a view in three directions while increasing the counter space in front of the sink—two good space expanders.

CENTER ATTRACTION *[opposite below]* Tucked into the shallow space behind a door, roomy storage shelves emphasize the prominence of the window. Note that the window appears more impressive than it really is—the opening in the shelves is larger than the window, revealing a portion of the gold-painted wall that acts as a border.

PHOTO ENTHUSIASTS [*right*] If you have more photos than table space, take a tip from this display. Trim the wall with two lengths of picture-hanging molding (the upper one turned upside down) spaced to hold a standard size photo between them. To remove a photo you need only bend it slightly and it comes out so another one can replace it.

DAINTY ADDITION [*opposite above*] The tiny guest room needs all the extra storage it can get. A narrow shelf about a foot below the ceiling holds accessories as well as plants that drape over its edge to soften the appearance of the cubbyhole-size room. The wall-mounted lamp frees the table for other uses.

OVERHEAD EXTRAS [*opposite below*] Store blankets and other linens inside cabinets mounted above the bathroom mirror. High enough not to interfere with activity at the counter, the glass-front cabinets are painted white to match the other woodwork.

ROOM AT THE TOP

Create space above eye level. Ceiling height is a funny thing—as long as the main portion of the ceiling is a standard height or higher, the eye doesn't seem to mind if part of it is lower. Indeed, the small lower part even makes the remainder seem higher in contrast, creating the effect of a tray-style ceiling.

This is a boon for anyone hoping to find extra storage or display space near the ceiling. As the examples on this page show, a few inches of space taken up for storage or display along the edge of the ceiling won't severely impact your perception of having enough headroom.

Other tricks, although not involving storage, will make the ceiling look taller too. Anything that draws interest to the ceiling, yet isn't darker than the walls, tends to expand the perceived height.

▶ **Place shallow false beams around the edge of and possibly across the room.** Paint the beams the same color as the walls and then paint the ceiling between the beams a lighter color or white. Although the beams are actually lower, the ceiling will seem higher because the walls appear taller.

▶ **Paint the ceiling to match the situation.** If a room is used mainly at night or usually has low light—a basement home theater, for instance—consider painting the ceiling midnight blue or another dark color. It will disappear and you won't be as conscious of overhead ductwork or other mechanical elements. Likewise if you want to create an infinitely romantic or imaginative treatment in a daytime room, paint the ceiling pale sky blue with wispy clouds.

chapter two
ROOM BY ROOM

Now that you've learned the basic principles of decorating small spaces, it's time to see how those principles can help solve typical dilemmas in every room. Incorporating the good ideas shown in this section will help you overcome space limitations in living rooms, dining areas, kitchens, bedrooms, baths, workstations, and even those odd little areas you've never considered particularly useful. Learning to take full advantage of extra space that already exists is one of the keys to successful decorating—and it's far less expensive than adding another room or buying a larger house.

The living room, despite having a name that identifies it as the center of family life, goes in and out of favor and up and down in size.

The Victorians entertained the preacher, but not the family, in the elegant front parlor, analogous to the living room. In the Fifties, the typical tract house had little common space other than a cramped living room and an eat-in kitchen—until the family added on the den. Next came the spacious great-room, which almost put the small, formal living room out of business. Now the living room is making a comeback, but less rigidly classified space lets a family use any area they like as their living room and decorate it as they choose.

So what kind of living room do you have? Is it a little too cozy? Does the space function the way you'd like? Does it seem large enough when you entertain? The diverse living rooms shown here are examples of rooms that make good use of available space while fitting the lifestyle of a particular family.

CASUAL AMBIENCE

Although it's on the small side, this living room makes a bow to style and casual sit-on-the-floor comfort. The main architectural feature is a well-lit storage wall with glass shelves and recesses painted in an accent color—the wall adds depth to the room and provides display space behind the sofa.

GOOD COMBINATION A wall of storage behind the sofa is a dominant element, yet takes up only one linear foot of floor space. Color, one of the most effective decorating tools in small spaces, turns the storage area into a showcase for favorite items. The painted recesses repeat the coral tone of the pillows, which are frequently used for seating on the floor.

A glass door provides a room-expanding outdoor view as well as light that floods the off-white room by day. Recessed canister fixtures illuminate the glass shelves at night, adding the drama of patterned light.

▶ *CARPET OR A RUG?* *Carpet provides a continuous surface that draws the eye from room to room—a good space-expanding trick, but only if it's all the same color. If floors are in good condition or if you need to anchor a furniture grouping, then choose a rug. You can also put an area rug on top of carpeting.*

NEOCLASSICAL ELEGANCE

This living room is part of an apartment that contains only 550 square feet—but that has immense style nonetheless. Vibrant gold walls ratchet up the energy level to produce a contemporary setting for neoclassical accessories. Aside from this one bold color, other furnishings are mainly subdued neutrals, but black accents seize attention in dramatic contrast to the golden walls. In this small space where every inch counts, a disciplined approach with furnishings results in a room with abundant personality and comfort too.

BOLD ACCENTS [*opposite* and *right*] Vertical elements—columns, candlesticks, and door moldings—pull the eye upward, a movement also stimulated by the vertical painting of a European monument. Even the map invites the eye to come in for a closer look. A round ottoman doubles as a coffee table in front of the plump sofa.

TEMPTING THE EYE [*right*] The unusual mirrored cabinet hides the television but offers an intriguing view of its own that makes the room seem larger.

▶ **ACCENT THE VERTICAL** *This phrase alone will help you make the right decorating choices. Lifting the eye to a higher plane helps overcome space limitations in a room by drawing attention to all the extra space above eye level. Without a reason to look upward, the eye essentially puts an artificial "ceiling" on the space, and it's even lower than the actual ceiling.*

CLEAR STATEMENTS

Two dissimilar living rooms share ideas that make each of the rooms seem larger. Both rooms take advantage of the main property of glass—its transparency—and use glass-top tables and large windows to expand the amount of visible space. A large floral-print fabric dominates in one room, and two smaller prints coexist in the other room.

GARDEN ARCHES [left]
Comfortable upholstered furniture, pastel shades, and oversize floral prints set a traditional tone. Two arched openings provide a vertical lift for the eye, leading it toward the framed painting and extra-wide crown molding. The shiny, glass Art Deco-style table adds a note of excitement while taking up almost no visual space.

UP-TO-DATE ANGLES [right]
Gleaming glass, lustrous wood flooring, and a ceiling-high accent wall form the backdrop for a collection of art and artifacts. The glass table echoes the rectangular shape of the unadorned window, and both are generous in scale, making the room appear more spacious. Fabric patterns are restrained and don't compete with each other.

COLOR PLUS

In each of these rooms, color, scale, and furniture arrangement are important. Color sets the mood, the scale and style of the furniture set the level of formality, and the arrangement determines traffic patterns. The two rooms have a lot in common, yet how much more different could living rooms be?

COLOR AND CHARACTER *[left]*
At first glance the room seems large. But look again—it's divided up into several much smaller areas, each arranged with its function in mind. There's an area for seating, anchored by an Oriental rug. A behind-the-sofa table also serves as a desk, with easy access to papers stored in the base cabinets. The storage wall holds the family library as well as stereo equipment. And despite the ample size of the furniture, none of it interferes with traffic patterns. Note the use of color too—bittersweet walls and a gold-tone ceiling warm the room considerably, yet are not so bright that they outshine its refined demeanor.

NEUTRAL, NATURALLY *[opposite]*
The bold scale of the furniture makes a definite statement, and its message is that naturals on all the furniture will make a small living room look bigger. An enormous ottoman serves as a coffee table and its honey-color, woven-straw texture works with the blinds to keep the room from being too sterile.

▶ **AMPLE LEGROOM** *The general guideline is that there should be from 12 to 18 inches of space between the sofa and the coffee table; an ottoman often sits closer to the sofa to make it easier to put your feet up.*

If eating is as natural as breathing, then why don't more homes have better dining areas? In older homes a spacious dining room was considered a necessity. As homes grow more compact and the emphasis shifts toward allocating more space to the family room or other areas, the number of square feet dedicated purely to eating is shrinking. At times there's only room for a breakfast bar with pull-up stools—not exactly a situation that inspires a family to share the day's experiences over a meal. It's up to you to make sure that your space works as hard as you do to keep your family happy and healthy. One way you can do this is to look at where you eat now and see if there are ways to improve it. Comfortable seating, the right type of table, and an expansive feeling can be achieved, even if your actual dining space is limited. Read on to find out how.

INFORMAL FORMALITY

Who says that you can't have formal dining unless you eat in a formal dining room? Formality, or a commitment to enjoying good food in the company of family and friends, is more about attitude than a rigid requirement for a special type of room. This is good because you may not even have a separate room for eating, or the one you have may be really small. Although your room may be a combination living room/dining room, or even an eat-in kitchen, you can create a gracious space for dining just the same.

CONVERSATIONAL STYLE A bay window in the living room offers the only spot for dining in this older home, yet the slim table is frequently the scene of elegant dinner parties. The comfortable banquette seats two people, and chairs from the living room pull up to the other sides. A narrow shelf wraps the window to display primitive masks, but can do double-duty as serving space if the table is pulled out.

▶ *SPACE-SAVING TABLES Investigate drop-leaf tables that fold down to become smaller when not being used for a crowd. If you have another nearby surface from which to serve food, you may be able to get by with a smaller-than-usual table for dining. In most situations, round tables will accommodate more people in less space than other shapes.*

GETTING INTO SHAPE

In a small kitchen a breakfast nook can be a marvelous thing—well-planned and attractive—or it can be a constant irritation that forces you to slide into a slot too small for a human body and sit on a hard, straight-back bench with elbows glued to your sides while you eat. Restaurants know that they can squeeze more people into less space when they line a wall with booths than if they use tables and chairs. So why is it that when you go to a restaurant, you like to sit in a booth, yet resist it in your own home? Could it be that your table is the wrong shape or size, or that there are better seating solutions?

CURVES AHEAD [opposite] It may be true that you can't put a square peg in a round hole, but a rounded bench definitely fits well in a square corner. Nestled into an angle formed by two tall windows, the bench creates an empty space behind it; adding a shelf to fill the gap creates an attractive niche for plants. Chairs provide more seating at the round table, which can always hold one or two extra people.

SQUARED OFF [right] A tabletop perched on a single pedestal allows plenty of legroom even for tall family members. Thick cushions on the three-sided, built-in bench are comfortable enough for diners to stay awhile, and if you need to pull up another chair, the square table has plenty of room. Painting the entire alcove, including the table, the light color of the walls produces a clean and simple effect that makes the room seem larger.

SCREEN THE VIEW

In the Far East where severe space limitations in the average home are a fact of life, the screen has long served a variety of purposes, yet it takes up almost no real space. A sliding shoji screen functions as a door to offer privacy, hide an unsightly area, or close off a room. A fixed screen defines an area or functions as a wall while still allowing light to come through. Take a tip from those who appreciate how useful screens can be and look around your house to see how a screen could help you manage your space.

EXPANSIVE VIEW *[right]* A solid wall cuts off any view and a completely open floor plan gives little definition, but a partially closed off space invites the curious eye to enter. Tall vertical supports open the space to the ceiling; fixed screens create a half-wall but don't block the line of sight above it. Notice the other screen that hides the light fixture in the display cabinet; repeating the screen element unifies the room and sets its very distinct style.

OUT OF SIGHT *[opposite]* Translucent screens on tracks slide open to provide easy access between the dining room and the kitchen, but they close to block the view of food preparation and for privacy at mealtime. Traditionally these screens were made of fragile paper, but today's versions are often made of far stonger materials.

SHOW-OFF SHELVING

Grandmother might have had a glass-door silver cabinet in her dining room or a special cabinet to display her good china. But because the manufacturer sized the furniture for a hypothetical dining room, grandmother was lucky to find a piece that fit where she wanted to put it. Today the notion that only a silver or china cabinet makes a fitting showcase for favorite serving pieces seems a little outdated. Built-ins—even those with ready-made components—can fit your space and blend well with other architectural features.

ALL EYES TOWARD THE CENTER
[left] Adjustable cubbies for serving pieces surround wall space deliberately left bare to focus attention on the painting. The cabinets beneath function both as a desk and a serving area. Grooved molding extends around the room to hold a collection of plates.

PERFECT FOR POTTERY
[opposite] Framed by wide moldings, the recessed cabinet with open shelves is almost flush with the wall. It borrows no floor space from the dining room, but it's an attention-grabbing display case for vintage serving pieces. Behind the closed doors more shallow shelves hold crystal and other slender items.

▶ **BUILD YOUR OWN** *Re-create the look of built-in shelving units by combining ready-made units and shelving or bookcases from a home improvement store. If your wall has enough support elsewhere, you can remove portions of the uprights and partially recess the unit into the wall. Trim and paint the front to match other moldings in the room.*

Even though its walls are stationary, a dining area must often expand or contract to fit varying numbers of people. The family might be eating alone or maybe you'll have guests, or sometimes there's a crowd so large that seating everyone around the table is out of the question. Because the room itself won't be changing, the furniture must. It's a given that living room chairs might be pulled into service in the dining room, but the table usually stays where it is. Here are some ways a small space and normal furniture can adapt to so many different situations.

TWICE AS USEFUL [right]
Stretching the length of the dining area, a slim and sophisticated wall-mounted wooden shelf is a natural buffet for serving crowds. The bonus: The area beneath it is open, so it takes up little visual space. In a pinch, younger members of the family enjoy using the shelf as a lunch counter while grown-ups dine at the main table.

REASONS FOR ROUND [opposite above] A round table is naturally convivial, inspiring easy conversation among everyone seated and always letting one more person squeeze in. It's also a good choice for most small dining rooms. Many round tables come with extra leaves for when the crowd comes for dinner, but these are removed for everyday use to create space around the table.

VERSATILE SERVER [opposite below] At parties the desk that occupies a few extra feet at the end of the room turns into an elegant server for dessert and coffee. This table goes from seating four to seating six with the addition of its leaf.

What comes to mind when you hear the word kitchen? Do you think of cooking supper for the family, that brief foray into gourmet soups, or long-ago afternoons spent on homework at the kitchen table? In the mind's eye the ideal kitchen can take on dimension and character befitting the pivotal role it so often plays: a cheerful, spacious room with sunlight streaming in, comfortable chairs around the family table, cookies in the oven, and birds singing outside the open window. In reality the typical kitchen is more likely to be somewhat cramped and perhaps have an unfriendly floor plan, too little counter space, or too little storage. So what can you do to bring your real kitchen more in line with your vision of what a good kitchen should be?

These kitchens and others throughout the book use creative space-enhancing principles to produce more functional and livable rooms. Let them inspire you with ideas to improve your kitchen and make the best use of your space.

CREATIVE CORNER

To an artistic individual, having room to display the things he or she most enjoys is almost as important as having food in the kitchen—it's food for the soul, so to speak. Tight space can leave little room for displaying favorite items and most stock cabinets aren't that creative. So what can you do to put your personal stamp on a small kitchen that's all too ordinary? Begin with color and add bold doses of the ones you love. Consider open shelving that shows off your favorite pieces. And let your personal taste be your main guide, because if you enjoy the way your kitchen looks, you'll enjoy being in there no matter what its size.

COLOR IT SPACIOUS
Red cabinets, Southwest-inspired shelf supports, and flagstone countertops identify this as the kitchen of an individualist. Open shelves let the eye travel to the wall (instead of stopping at a cabinet-door barrier), which adds about 15 inches of apparent width to the upper part of the room.

HIGH-ALTITUDE STORAGE

Every year there's a crop of new products and gadgets, each one promising to help you prepare food faster, cook better, clean up quicker, or surround yourself with the shiniest floors in town. Chances are you'd also like to buy a few pretty plates or upgrade utensils. But where would you put new items?

Because improved products come along all the time, a kitchen is the perfect place to use every storage trick in the book. If you've run out of space in the usual places, then look overhead for more. In addition to pot racks and below-the-ceiling shelves, put cabinet tops to work. Stash small items you don't use often in containers such as lidded baskets or fabric-covered boxes stacked on top of the cabinets. If the boxes match your walls or blend with the cabinetry, they'll look like part of the architecture and will keep the room looking tidy.

CLOSE AT HAND [*right*] Cutting out a portion of the ceiling for a skylight also opens up a world of storage possibilities. Brass rods along two sides hold S-hooks for easy access to hanging pots and pans. The pull-out cutting board masquerades as a drawer when not in use.

TALL ORDER [*opposite*] Extending the upper cabinets to the ceiling adds almost 50 percent to their storage capacity. A long display shelf above the cased opening ties the two sides of the room together with one clean, unbroken line, and the expanded view goes all the way to the outside.

▶ *ORGANIZATIONAL EXTRAS To make the most of space in existing cabinets, check out some of the latest storage aids. Wire racks, plastic bins and baskets, airtight containers, pull-out trash cans and towel racks, plus other products help minimum cabinet space store the maximum amount.*

CROWD PLEASER *[above left]* Adding a butcher-block top to a roomy base cabinet creates a hardworking kitchen island that is a favorite gathering place as well. The butcher block extends over the cabinet on two sides so family and friends can pull up a seat or help prepare food.

DEEP STORAGE *[below left]* Roomy drawers and shelves on the other sides store kitchen essentials. A recessed kickboard prevents items from rolling beneath the island.

TINY TITAN *[opposite above]* This small island packs a lot of useful features into very few square feet. It holds a small microwave oven (there's a floor plug beneath) and shallow shelves for storing spices. Another shelf at floor level holds baskets of staples and the top is large enough to prepare food.

BAKER'S PRIDE *[opposite below left]* Cool marble is the ideal work surface for baking and candymaking, according to many chefs. This table works as an extra countertop and is used for dining or serving too.

SPACE-SAVING TABLE *[opposite below right]* An interesting old table adds an antique character to this kitchen while lending counter space as well. Casters make simple work of moving the table from spot to spot or even into adjoining rooms for serving at parties.

ISLAND HOPPING

You may have considered installing a practical island in the middle of your kitchen and then decided that you didn't want to suffer through the remodeling process. Well, it's time to think again. The islands on these pages offer extra work surfaces, places to eat, and in some cases, plenty of storage, yet not one of them involved remodeling.

If you need an island built to an exact size, have it made off-site in a cabinet shop and then move it into the kitchen when it's complete.

FORM & FUNCTION

This kitchen and breakfast room, reflecting the
Arts and Crafts (or Mission-style) Movement of
the early 20th century, shows influences that go far
beyond that deliberately simple style. A basic tenet
of the movement was that everything in a room
should fulfill some useful purpose or it shouldn't be
there at all. In a fairly small kitchen, where function
and storage are so important, this means that
everything must work together.

BONUS SPACE [opposite above] The hinged top of each bench lifts to reveal hidden storage inside. This is an especially handy spot for little-used appliances or seasonal decorations. Thick cushions on top of each bench make for far more comfortable seating than bare wood.

USING EVERY INCH [opposite below] Benches on two sides of the breakfast table provide plenty of seating while taking up a minimum of floor space. Upper cabinets fit into a shallow space beside the window, but there's enough counter space beneath to display cookbooks or serve food.

WINDING PATH [above] Straight lines detour to allow room to walk by the sink cabinet. The shallow counter on the left is still roomy enough for food preparation and serving. Glass-pane doors and wall-to-wall windows extend the view, which dramatically increases the feeling of space.

IDEAS FOR EVERY INCH

Part of the fun of decorating small spaces is thinking of creative ways to use every cubic inch. Traffic, for instance, can be a major problem if it cuts right through the room; unless you control the flow, it eats up a lot of the little space your kitchen has. Carving out enough counter space is also a challenge. Stoves, refrigerators, and sinks need work areas beside them, but sometimes it's not available, or is simply too small to be useful. Building short walls to route traffic, rearranging existing cabinets, or extending countertops are much less expensive options than completely remodeling, so analyze the space you have and figure out the best way to get the results you need.

SELF-SERVE COUNTERS
[opposite above] Sleek stainless-steel countertops take advantage of spaces high and low. One is used as a coffee center and the other, above the taller cabinets, is a buffet server.

COOKBOOK LIBRARY *[opposite below left]* In another view of the same kitchen, cabinets and shelves fit into a nook, creating a broad counter convenient to the stove. Wide doors permit access to items in the back corner.

CLOSE AT HAND *[opposite below right]* Several skillets hang conveniently above the stove on a rack that also holds condiments for cooking. A shallow shelf wends its way around the room near the ceiling to display vintage plates and collectibles.

GREAT DIVIDE *[left]* In a city kitchen where entertaining is a way of life, a narrow sliver of raised countertop above the sink is only wide enough for guests to enjoy a drink and a snack, but it also acts as a divider to help traffic stay out of the kitchen.

A bedroom is a private place, that sanctuary of solitude where you can go at the end of the day—and it's completely yours. Here you can unwind and read a book with your feet up, or sit and do nothing—in the lotus position. Or pretend to be a star and eat bonbons while reclining in a velvet robe. But no matter what activities you enjoy, chances are good that you'd be happy if your bedroom had a little more space.

Like bedrooms, most closets aren't as large as they probably should be. Even the generous walk-in closet that convinced you to buy the house is now packed with four seasons' worth of clothes, but the ones you want are lost because they're so squeezed together. Imagine what having a larger closet would be like.

Next let your mind picture your bath. Is it basically functional but a little outdated? Does it need more storage and maybe a facelift?

Imagining the possibilities is fun, but small spaces don't change by themselves—you'll need to help them change. With the ideas in this chapter, you'll soon be able to go from dreams to reality, and just imagine how you'll enjoy your home then!

CLEVER SOLUTION

Structural features such as poorly placed light switches, windows, vents, doorways, and even ductwork can interfere with your sense of design as you find yourself forced to arrange furniture to suit the room's limitations.

Try viewing those annoying little quirks as an opportunity for a creative solution—and you may be surprised at how they can fire your imagination! Fill in the area beneath ductwork with premade cabinets (see *left*) or build out the wall with actual closets. Go ahead and place furniture over a vent, but use one of the adjustable plastic vent deflectors to reroute the air. Consider replacing the door with one that hinges on the opposite side for better placement when it's open, or design a window treatment that disguises the actual size of the window. Sometimes the solution to a difficult situation is so attractive that you'll almost forget it started out as a problem.

KING-SIZE CUBBYHOLE
Ductwork taking up space along the ceiling was the inspiration for a clever storage solution. Tall cabinets create a perfect niche for the bed and lights above eliminate the need for additional bedside lamps.

BONUS STORAGE

In times past if someone wanted to keep something in a handy, yet safe place, they hid it under the mattress. Times have changed but the need for accessible storage is as relevant as ever. Some of the most underused cubic feet in the room are those beneath the bed.

Many platform beds have drawers or shelves for built-in storage beneath the mattress; these are available in every size, from king-size for grownups to bunk beds for kids. If you prefer a more traditional style, then look for matching baskets or underbed boxes for dust-free storage of clothing or other items. If your bed frame is too low to accommodate baskets, raise it with casters or consider purchasing a frame with taller legs.

DOUBLE SOLUTION *[opposite]* Storage drawers and shelves in a sleek platform under the bed eliminate the need for a separate chest of drawers. A translucent wall of glass windows behind the bed separates it from an area with higher traffic, creating more privacy and better traffic flow.

BASKETS OF BASICS *[above right]* Put space beneath the bed to good use with handsome storage baskets that tuck beneath the bed frame. Cover them with a floor-length dust ruffle or let the baskets show for an up-to-date and stylish look.

STACKS OF STORAGE *[below right]* Cabinets and cubicles store all sorts of overflow in the guest room, yet none of it interferes with comfort. Use stock base cabinets, a finished countertop, and plank shelving and adjust the height of the cabinets to conform to the ceiling if necessary.

ATTIC HIDEAWAYS

Rather than presenting a dilemma, attic room features like dormer windows and unusual angles add character to the room and offer opportunities for hidden storage. Story-and-a-half houses have their second story tucked under the eaves from the inception, but like finished attics, they often have short walls (called knee walls) at the sides.

Place the head of the bed against a knee wall (see the photo on *pages 78–79*) or tuck the side of the bed beneath the slope, provided there's enough room to sit and read in bed.

Add window seats with storage beneath dormer windows or, if windows are wide enough, line them with shelves. Space behind the knee walls is ideal for storage too. Provide access either through short doors or install recessed cabinets or drawers with fronts flush with the wall.

PERFECT SYMMETRY *[opposite]* Twin headboards fit neatly at the end of an attic bedroom. Small halogen lamps direct focused light toward the beds, without large shades that take up space and block the view.

TRIPLE TREAT *[below]* This attic-turned-dormitory accommodates several overnight guests at a time. An identical wall-mounted lamp at the head of each bed eliminates the need for bedside tables, freeing floorspace.

ROOM TO GROW

As much as you'd like for your little ones to remain small forever, they have a way of growing bigger almost overnight. The room that was so delightful when he or she was an infant won't suit a youngster who's playing with trucks or building houses out of blocks. Plenty of space for toys isn't a luxury—it's a necessity for Mom's sanity—yet in many kids' rooms, storage is an afterthought.

SHIPSHAPE STORAGE [opposite] Stacked drawers and roomy cabinets offer storage for both clothing and toys while creating a colorful and sturdy base for the raised bed. The cabinets continue to the ceiling to form the ends of the bed; they also store large and out-of-season items for Mom.

STORY TIME [top right] Beneath the dormer window a small seat has a comfortable cushion and drawers for books and games.

SLEEPOVER GUEST [bottom right] The bottom row of drawers is actually a single drawer that pulls out on casters to reveal another mattress.

▶ **CHOOSING COLORS** Kids thrive on colors that stimulate creativity. Choose a bright pastel for the walls and either extend it to furniture (to make the room seem more spacious) or switch to another bright color that complements the walls. It's easy to clean little fingerprints if you choose gloss or semigloss paint.

NAP TIME OR PLAYTIME

With only one new piece of furniture, you can add a second story to your child's bedroom and create a cheerful playroom that will thrill your son or daughter. Instead of furnishing the bedroom with a regular bed that takes up the floor space, substitute a bed built above the usual height. Put the space beneath it to work as a playhouse, fort, or all-around playroom and furnish it accordingly.

CHILD-SIZE STORAGE *[opposite]* Stackable cubes are an ideal system for storing toys and books at a child's own eye level. Add more sections as the child grows taller or move them to a closet and use them for sweaters. Use the space beneath a window as a seat for reading or storytelling; just make a soft cushion to fit the empty space (or a bench in front of the window) and add a few extra throw pillows.

IMAGINATION STATION *[top right]* Playmates spend countless hours in this little playhouse beneath the bed, where tiny tables and chairs share space with toys and teddy bears. The end of the raised bed is a versatile ladder that at times serves as Rapunzel's tower or a pirate ship's rigging.

CLEANUP CORNER *[bottom right]* In many countries—most of Europe, for instance—it's common to see a lavatory in the bedroom because this is an area where one spends a lot of time. A corner sink in a child's room makes easy work of washing little hands and may even postpone the need for an extra bathroom. This sink has a fabric skirt to cover items stored beneath it.

EXPANDING THE BATH

Almost every bath has moments when it seems too cramped for comfort, sometimes because the room really isn't large enough or your spouse is crowding your space. To create the feeling, if not the actuality, of more space, use mirrors—framed, unframed, wall-size, or something smaller.

WALL OF MIRROR *[opposite above]* Using a wall-to-wall mirror at one end of this deep-tone, narrow bath increases the apparent size enough to keep the room from feeling too close for comfort. Surrounding the mirror with a frame gives it the look of furniture (to attach wood molding strips, use the glue made for reattaching automobile rear view mirrors).

LIGHT AND A VIEW *[opposite below]* With only one wall available, both the mirror and a glass-block window must share the space, but the solution works very well. The framed mirror is large enough for seeing how you look, and the textured glass blocks let in plenty of daylight but maintain privacy without any window treatment.

THE IMPOSTERS *[above left]* Only the small opening in the center is a real window—the two look-alikes on the sides are actually mirrors reflecting the room. A skylight adds light to compensate for the small window.

TWIN ARCHES *[above right]* A large arched mirror greatly increases the perceived size of the room. Hidden tube lighting behind the matching tiled opening increases the illusion of depth.

HEIGHTENED IMPACT *[below left]* A dramatic mirror that climbs to the peak of the vaulted ceiling makes the bath appear far larger than it really is. A little extra space at the end of the tub is an attractive display for artwork, plants, or bath-time necessities.

STORAGE NOOKS

Using every little slice of space in a bath often makes the difference between a room that's too cramped for comfort and one that you truly enjoy using. Towels and bed linens take up a lot of storage space, yet today's bath must also have room for the latest in hair- and skin-care products, small appliances, and numerous other items your grandparents never imagined. When space is already tight, where can you squeeze out the extra storage you need? Here are some spots you may not have considered.

AT THE ENTRANCE [*above left*]
A formerly unused bit of space outside the bath now forms a dramatic entrance. Glass tops on thick miniwalls create display pedestals for special perfumes, flowers, or sculpture. A glass shelf over the mirror offers additional storage space.

IN THE WALL [*center left*]
Balanced with precision on casters, a ceiling-height shelf unit rolls out from a sliver of space beside the vanity. Although the unit moves easily, sides on the shelves keep bottles and other containers from falling.

OVER THE TANK [*below left*]
Extend the top of the vanity to provide extra shelf space for plants or toiletries. Cover the new shelf to match the vanity, and attach it to the wall with L-brackets or hinges so that you can move it for emergency access to plumbing.

AROUND THE CORNERS
[*opposite*] A pair of tall corner cabinets, each with one side angled, stores bathroom essentials and linens in drawers and on shelves. A shelf above the pedestal sink offers a much-needed extra surface.

Ideally a house is stylish and functional, with convenient work centers that actually help you do your work. This used to mean only the kitchen—still arguably the most important—but other work centers are almost as essential to today's busy families.

With the advent of computers, printers, and all the other accessories needed, a home office has become one of life's little necessities. It's frequently used by all the family members, including youngsters.

The laundry room, too, is changing, as economy-size containers and recycling bins join washers and dryers in sharing the space. And then you need a spot to make coffee, some place to pursue your hobbies, and space for the electronic equipment, which now has an entourage of videos, DVDs, and CDs. How can it all fit in only the space you have?

A house must change with the times to be functional, so this chapter deals with all the minor work centers where you spend productive time. Good organization can help fit more into less space, and you'll feel happier as a result.

MOVING UP

Proving that every little bit of space can be used, this strikingly sophisticated office is in a loft room at the head of the stairs. Figuring out how to gain access to the nearby rooftop garden required some innovative thinking, but the resulting gain in storage was clearly worth the effort.

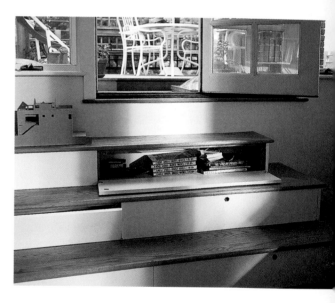

STEPS TO STORAGE [opposite]
This small office tucked into the loft has room for a desk (a door set on file cabinets), lots of storage, a desk chair, and even comfortable seating for two guests. A system of shelves topped with treads functions as storage and steps—the front risers fold forward for access to the space within. In addition to bookshelves, the waist-high wall, a ledge, and the beams above are pulled into service to display a collection of paper sculptures. Daylight coming through glass doors and windows reflects from the off-white surfaces inside. At night spotlights on the ceiling beams do the job.

FOLD-DOWN SOLUTION [above]
Each of the risers on this extra-wide staircase is a pair of cabinet doors, hinged at the bottom to fold forward when open. Inside is space for office essentials and a lot more storage besides. The solid treads are safely supported for use as steps and can display art, plants, or other favorite items.

SPARE CORNERS

If there's the slightest bit of extra space in a corner, by all means—put it to use! If you connect the new area with shelving or cabinets in the room, it will look as though you planned the corner feature all along. These hardworking corners create new space for paying bills, working at the computer, organizing a home office, or even making coffee. What could you do in your house?

TIME OUT *[opposite]* Go sit in the corner when it's time to jot down a note, pay bills, or make a phone call. A triangular table may be all the room you need. Shallow shelves take up only a few inches of space above the desk, but store plenty of useful items.

COMPUTER GARAGE *[above right]* Tall cabinets can't extend all the way to the wall because of the window, but the empty space leaves room for a mini office. A dining chair does double duty at the desk, and drawers store files and household papers. The flexible tambour door rolls down to hide the computer and the paperwork inside for a neater appearance.

MULTITASKING *[center right]* The clean-lined desk and shelves clinging to the corner are part of a basement office. One wall has a panel system for displaying pictures, and another table adds even more work space.

START THE DAY *[below right]* A cabinet dedicated to the art of making breakfast is a true indulgence, but so handy in this day of eat-and-run. This one is in a kitchen, but it could just as easily be in a dressing room or closet for easy morning access. With a pull-out counter, lift-up top, and electrical outlets in back, it's easily accessible for those with eyes only half open.

LAUNDRY SPACEMAKERS

Next to the kitchen, the laundry room is the workhorse of the home. The storage ideas on these pages represent the ideal; unusual features, such as the slide-out laundry shelf and drop-down detergent bin, may require working with a custom cabinet company or your builder to devise solutions that fit your home. Other ideas you can implement using stock cabinetry and shower rods.

HOBBY HIDEAWAY [above left] Another counter and a few extra storage drawers convert part of the laundry room to space for Mom's crafts or Dad's lures.

LAUNDRY TAMERS [above] A basket for each family member's clothes, hanging space, storage cabinets, and a handy shelf directly over the washer keep the laundry room neat all the time.

IN THE BIN [left] Store detergent, pet food, or items to recycle in a large bin made with a plastic trash can attached to a fold-out door. The door is a standard cabinet door hinged at the bottom instead of the side.

EXTRA HELPER [opposite above] A larger surface frequently comes in handy when folding stacks of laundry. This custom-built pull-out shelf is similar to pull-out butcher-block drawers available for kitchen cabinetry.

CONVENIENCE UNDERGROUND [opposite below] A cheerful basement utility room has an extra-long counter that extends over a small freezer, then drops down to desk height to hold a computer. Cabinets hold mesh storage bins, while other supplies go behind the undersink curtain. Yellow paint minimizes the effect of plumbing pipes against the unfinished ceiling.

ORGANIZED WORKSHOP

Creative juices bubble up easily when you have a space dedicated to your craft, whatever it may be. Shelves and bookshelves convert easily to storage units for fabric or crafts supplies that are stashed in decorative boxes or bins, but don't overlook the repurposing possibilities of other furniture pieces too. Anything with drawers or doors can tidily store your stuff; use smaller boxes and bins inside each drawer or on each shelf to keep items organized. For a movable work surface with storage, consider a tool cart on locking casters or a utility workbench from a home improvement center. Have plywood or shelving cut to fit the top of the tool cart to provide a work surface.

QUILTER'S DREAM *[opposite]*
A bank of shelves that stores everything out in the open holds fabrics arranged by color. Counters at different heights, some for sitting and using tools and some for standing, line the wall beneath the window.

PLACES FOR EVERYTHING
[right] A central island on locking casters is a useful addition because it can be moved aside if necessary. Portable pull-out baskets are even handier than drawers and are filled with plastic boxes for smaller items.

▶ **OTHER WORKROOM IDEAS** *Cover walls with pegboard or cork to hang tools or pictures for inspiration. • Paint the walls a color that makes you happy. • Provide good lighting even if you have sunshine. • Stack identical labeled boxes beneath the countertop. • Include a folding table or rolling cart. • Have an easy-to-mop floor, chairs on casters, and storage for reference books or patterns.*

One of the charms of an older home is that it probably has many interesting nooks and crannies that are fun to explore. Tucked under the eaves or hidden away in a closet, there's almost no telling what you might find. Well, get out your hat and a magnifying glass—become a detective to find some unused nooks in your own house!

Check the closets and stairwells and then move on to the attic and the garage. Look under the sink and by the back door. You're unlikely to discover a secret wall or hidden passageway, but you may decide there's enough unused space to create some surprises yourself—and your sleuthing efforts will reward you by making your home seem more spacious.

ART EXHIBIT

Art lovers, like antiques collectors, have an almost predictable dilemma. A lifetime spent learning to recognize good design and fine craftsmanship—and trying to obtain those special pieces that touch something deep within—often ends up with the house too full and space running out!

Short of parting with pieces in the collection, the answer is to find someplace to put them. Here's a situation where converting a closet to a different purpose creates an extraordinary display case.

FIRESIDE GALLERY This little closet was too close to the fireplace, too far from the front door, and too shallow for hanging clothes. Covering the back wall with a mirror, adding sturdy glass shelves, and changing to glass-paned double doors makes all the difference in the way it functions. Now it's a showcase for pottery and glassware—a focal point in the elegant room.

FARAWAY VIEW *[opposite]* Black and white travel photos sail down a curving ocean blue wall to reach a curved ledge attached at the corner. For unity choose identical mats and frames, and use a level and plumb line to help you keep them straight.

HIGH PLATEAU *[above right]* Finding a spot for a horizontal painting is easier in a stairway than in a room with only narrow stretches of wall space. Hang the painting above narrow shelves for other objects, but be sure that everything is high enough not to be knocked off. One guideline is to place the top item at eye level for the upper floor.

STAFFORDSHIRE & STORAGE *[center right]* Hanging fragile plates on the stairway wall isn't such a good idea, but displaying them on a landing creates a nice focal point in a hard-to-decorate area. Note the storage along the wall too: Full-size doors conceal closets that slope back into formerly unused attic space.

TABLE EXTENSION *[below right]* A vase of flowers on a narrow table is a nice little surprise for stairclimbers and also makes use of the mysterious extension built at the top of the stairs. The mirror above it functions as a window, reflecting light from the skylight.

STAIRWAY PRESENTATION

When the rest of the house is desperate for more space, it seems somehow unfair that the stairway wall is so broad and tall that its very size is intimidating. Should you hang a huge painting that dwarfs other artwork? (Yes, if you like.) Or would it be best to ignore it and learn to enjoy plain paint? (Yes, that's an option too.) And then there's that space at the top—what was the builder thinking? Every situation is different, but here are some interesting ways to decorate the stairway and find a place for extra items at the same time.

DIVIDING WALL

Subdividing an already modest-size space with a new wall? Yes! It's a tried and true way to reroute traffic that cuts through the room and even make extra space! Consider this: Because of traffic patterns, there's often an invisible hall going through the room—by rerouting the traffic through an intentional corridor, you can keep it from interfering with furniture placement. For example, a slim wall behind a bed can help you carve out a spot for the mini office or crafts area you've always wanted. Let these examples inspire you.

THE WELL-TRAVELED SIDE
[opposite] Traffic to the dressing room is channeled alongside a curving display wall with large cubbyholes that contain a sculpture collection.

THE PRIVATE SIDE *[above right]* The bed backs up to the other side of the dividing wall. Even though it doesn't reach all the way to the ceiling, the wall effectively creates a private sanctuary.

ANOTHER APPLICATION *[below right]* Allocating space for a bedroom and a bath in one small attic requires some creative arranging. A partial-height wall eliminates the need for separate rooms with doors. In the bath a square tub with a shower fits under the dormer window and its glass door won't restrict the light or a view of the outside.

► **MORE STORAGE** *Mount a shallow cabinet with doors in the space near the back door and use it to store cleaning supplies, spices, or other items frequently needed in the kitchen. Extend a wall-to-wall shelf over the window and the top of the cabinet for storage of larger items.*

BACKDOOR BONUS

C oming and going through the back door as many times as you do, you're likely to pass through the space without giving it a second thought. Muddy boots and baseball gloves stashed in the corner might draw attention, but if you use the area only to feed the dog, you may be ignoring its great potential.

Use the familiar space to create an attractive second entrance with room for those things that will probably end up there anyway. This is one spot your family sees often, so make it as nice as the rest of your home.

PLEASANT CHANGE *[left and opposite]* Formerly a messy catchall for coats and boots, the back entrance is now a cheerful room that inspires neatness (which never hurts in a small space). A coatrack, a pantry cabinet, and ample overhead storage help keep things in order.

The narrow slab of marble beneath the window serves as a convenient potting bench or a butler's pantry to handle kitchen overflow when necessary. The fabric skirt beneath it hides all kinds of things—from potting soil to canning jars but someone passing through never has to know.

chapter three
WHOLE HOUSES

A house is made up of rooms containing space—and that space can be organized to fit the needs of the people who live there. As you look at the photographs in this chapter, you'll see whole homes decorated in different styles. On closer observation you'll also see that they have a lot in common. Each of them is a good example of using established guidelines to produce a house that lives larger than it is. By the time you finish this chapter, you'll know how to begin with the principles, use them in every room, and create a space-savvy home in any style that suits your tastes. Your home will function better and look more beautiful too.

Clean lines, classic furniture, the extensive use of white, and daylight pouring through simply clad windows are the hallmarks of this house. Formerly cut up into dark, too-small rooms, the new and more open floor plan suits a young lifestyle much better.

The house holds the line on simplicity in every room with a no-color color scheme and only minimal touches of accent colors. Pared-down furnishings are adequate, but careful editing has eliminated all excess. Dark wood floors keep the rooms grounded, in gleaming contrast to the space-expanding all-white walls and ceilings.

In the main room—a combined kitchen, dining area, and living room—two walls work especially hard. At one end base cabinets, appliances, and the sink create the kitchen area; at the other, a wall-to-wall bank of cabinets rising almost to the ceiling holds everything imaginable in neatly organized compartments. Between them a storage island with a marble top and a dining table mirror each other's massive rectangular shapes. Subdued rugs define specific areas: The dining table and chairs sit on an Oriental carpet and slipcovered chairs in the seating area are anchored by a flokati rug. Broad expanses of glass offer room-expanding views of the deck, often used as a secondary living room.

WHITE ON WHITE *[above]*
Comfortably slipcovered seating in this area is as pristinely white as the rest of the room. The only accents are black; they rescue the area from being too pale but don't add color of their own. The large, low, sculptural coffee table accommodates guests who like to sit casually on the floor, but its free-form glass top takes up little visual space.

MINIMAL FURNITURE *[opposite]*
A sturdy wooden table serves multiple functions: It's used for dining, playing games, or any activities that require a lot of work surface. The retro-style aluminum chairs, which mimic the brushed-steel finish of kitchen appliances, easily move into other areas when needed. Wall-to-wall storage cabinets corral clutter behind a neat facade.

NATURAL LIGHT [*right*] Two windows in the sink wall add to the abundant light that floods the room; one has frosted glass for privacy and the other has an adjustable blind, both minimal window treatments that help to maximize the space in the room. Open shelving, unlike cabinets with doors, reveals space all the way to the wall. All-white cabinets have convenient features such as a pull-out cutting board.

GALLEY KITCHEN [*opposite*] One wall holds the appliances, which are separated from the storage island by a walkway wide enough for several people to work at the same time. Thick slabs of marble, an ideal surface preferred by many serious cooks, top both the kitchen cabinets and the island. A vaulted ceiling lifts the eye for a dramatic increase in the sense of space, and the skylight and glass sliders bathe the whole room in light and fresh air.

▶ **ONE AND ONLY** *To instantly unify rooms, paint walls, ceilings, and trim with one color of paint. Use the same paint to camouflage mismatched wooden furniture that you'd like to make disappear and to coordinate accessories such as frames and storage boxes.*

PRINCIPLES AT WORK

▶ **COLOR AND PATTERN** Minimal color and pattern make the rooms seem larger because there is no dominant element to stop the eye from traveling. Mismatched chairs and a stool have white slipcovers to unify them. A few pastel accents, plus black, are the only departures from basically all-white rooms, but plenty of texture keeps the decorating from seeming too sterile for comfort.

▶ **ARRANGEMENT AND SCALE** The furniture is large and informal, but there are very few pieces: slipcovered chairs, a couple of big tables, metal chairs in the dining room and bedroom, a bed, and a few pieces painted white to match the walls—plus built-in storage. A rug anchors each group of furniture to define its separate identity.

▶ **STORAGE** One wall of almost ceiling-height cabinets holds a maximum amount while taking up only minimal square footage along the edge of the room. White paneled doors hide items stored inside, creating a neat appearance and adding another textured element.

▶ **ILLUSION** Large expanses of glass let in light and expand the view to include the outside. Because there's only a transparent division between the house and the deck, they are viewed as one continuous space, which is far larger than the actual space inside the house. The glass-top coffee table and the wire-mesh chair almost disappear.

▶ **CONVERSIONS** Adding a row of Shaker pegs to a narrow hallway lets it function as a closet for heavy coats and hats. Slipcovers sewn from one fabric turn mismatched chairs into a matched set.

▶ **BETTER USE OF SPACE** Opening up three small rooms to become one large room does away with the barrier of walls and creates more livable space. Using sliding glass doors instead of French doors frees more floor space for furniture. Well-defined zones for eating, cooking, and conversation create smooth traffic patterns.

PALE ACCENTS *[opposite]* A room can stick to its basically all-white color scheme, yet still have plenty of texture. Quilted fabric, woven storage baskets, and a lamp with a spherical paper shade add interest to this bedroom. Small doses of color—shell pink pillows and black and white photos in a natural frame—keep the white from being too stark. The framed photos create a strong horizontal element that exaggerates the width of the room and lifts the eye too.

OUTDOOR ACCESS *[above]* Sliding doors in both the bedroom and the main room lead to the deck. If French doors had been used, open doors would have taken up valuable floor space, while these doors leave it free and clear. An extra-long rod allows curtains with grommets to slide freely to the sides, where they don't obstruct the view. The wire-mesh chair and footstool offer a place to sit but have little visual weight and seem to disappear.

▶ **EASY CHANGES** *To keep all-white or neutral upholstery and bed linens from being boring, add a few accessories, such as pillows, in one or two accent colors. To revive your color scheme or change the look for different seasons, replace the pillow covers.*

PRIVACY SCREEN *[opposite]*
Large pots of bamboo offer solitude and seclusion from other houses in the closely built neighborhood. The gray deck is a soothing backdrop for outdoor furniture painted white to match interior furnishings. Wide steps provide extra seating for a crowd at outdoor gatherings.

GOT IT PEGGED *[above left]* A row of simple Shaker pegs makes good use of limited space along a narrow hallway. The pegs are above eye level for safety's sake, but hats and coats still hang at a convenient height for adults.

UPDATED CLASSIC *[above right]*
Bridging the years to reflect the original style of the house, the pedestal sink is a new addition. A round mirror amplifies light from the window. The louvered closet doors flanking the doorway add much-needed texture to the all-white rooms.

OPEN HOUSE *[below right]* The small L-shape house opens to a spacious deck and a broad expanse of lawn visible from several rooms. Large panes of glass provide unobstructed views of the outside and, with the skylight, admit plenty of air and light.

A 1920s bungalow (containing less than 800 square feet), a preference for budget retro furniture and rich colors, and a refusal to stick to traditional furniture placement all add up to a vibrant house that nods to the past as well. Color is the main principle at work here—the deep-toned walls seem to recede at night, which is when these rooms are occupied. During the day the large windows let in plenty of light. Simultaneously the green and rust color scheme draws the eye from room to room with its repetition of slightly different shades. The colors form a contrasting backdrop for the oversize, mostly neutral furniture and light-tone accessories. In the kitchen open shelves increase both actual and perceived space, while mirrors throughout the house work hard to expand the view.

CHARMING BUNGALOW

[opposite below] Buying a too-small house in a desirable neighborhood creates a classic dilemma because although it's in the right place, the house requires some space-expanding tricks to make it livable. Remaining true to the integrity of the architecture and furnishing it with an eye toward increasing the perceived space results in a house that lives larger than its actual size.

RELAXING RETREAT *[left]*

Encouraging the eye to travel between areas, the dining room wall color repeats in the living room in smaller doses—a pillow, lampshade, and the fireplace wall (shown on *pages 150–151*). Instead of its back facing the dining table, the oversize sofa is on the diagonal and extends slightly into the dining room, opening up more space in the center of the living room. The garage sale table had a marred top, but its new faux-leather upholstered top converts it to a functional ottoman/coffee table. The large-scale display cabinet would seem too massive were it not for glass doors and shelves that seem to disappear.

OVERSIZE EMPHASIS All eyes go to the energetic pumpkin orange fireplace wall, a focal point that distracts from the small size of the living room. On the poplar mantel, an enormous letter salvaged from an old building demands immediate attention. The remaining walls relax into deep green, a color that contrasts well with the oak floors, orange wall, and neutral furniture. Yellow flowers, other yellow accents, and light wood tones keep the color scheme lively and prevent darker colors from seeming dull.

STEPPED UP STORAGE [right] A new vanity, assembled from stock components and a few extra pieces of wood, increases the storage capacity of the bath and adds much-needed counter space with an extension over the toilet. Mirrors on each side make up for the basin placed directly beneath a window. The olive green on the vanity and rust on the ceiling and upper walls repeat the color scheme used in every room.

VARIATION ON A THEME [opposite] Sage green walls in the kitchen are a gentler version of the green used elsewhere. Open shelving, used instead of cabinets along the wall, increases the perception of space because the eye can travel farther. The retro dresser, matching the bedroom furniture, stores serving pieces, silverware, and table linens in the breakfast area. Notice the framed mirror leaning against the wall; it creates the illusion of seeing into the next room.

▶ *INSTANT RESULTS Expand the size of your room immediately by leaning a mirror against the wall. Adjust the tilt to achieve different reflections. Try placing a mirror under upper cabinets, over a buffet or desk, opposite a window, or in the corner of the bedroom. For even more interest combine a couple of mirrors in different sizes, offsetting them slightly to reflect different views.*

PRINCIPLES AT WORK

▶ **COLOR AND PATTERN** Assertive colors drawn from a palette of pumpkin orange, green, brown, and yellow are the key to why the rooms in this house flow together so well. The eye naturally travels from a room with pumpkin walls, for instance, into the next room where there's a pillow in the same color. Most of the furniture is upholstered in neutral fabric, with the exception of some '50s-era chairs that are in the same range of orange, green, brown, and yellow.

▶ **ARRANGEMENT AND SCALE** Using extra-large furnishings in a small space works well if only a limited number of pieces are used. The over-scale sofa and ottoman don't seem too big for the living room because they're placed on the diagonal, expanding the boundaries of the room by borrowing space from the dining room. An enormous metal letter is the dominant element on the pumpkin orange accent wall, where it heightens the wall's impact. In the bedroom the dresser along the window wall is suitable only because its large mirror reflects so much natural light; in effect, it replaces the window it covers.

▶ **STORAGE** Open shelves and cubes in the kitchen expand the line of sight to the wall instead of stopping it at cabinet doors. In the bath a new mirrored cabinet and a shelf that extends over the toilet provide extra storage for bath items.

▶ **ILLUSION** Mirrors take the place of windows, offering amplified light and an expanded view of the room.

▶ **MULTIPURPOSE FURNITURE** Upholstering the top of a marred table so it serves as an ottoman is a good example of adapting furniture to suit new needs. Using a bedroom dresser in the breakfast room to provide storage for table linens and a convenient surface for serving food is another example.

TOO LITTLE WALL SPACE
The furniture placement here is unconventional, brought about in part by the sheer size of the furniture and the room's many doors and windows. Placing the retro dresser on the only wall long enough meant covering a window with the mirror, but the reflection keeps the room from feeling too dark and cramped. On another wall the bed sits directly beneath a window with diamond-shape panes that serve as a decorative headboard. Deep rust walls again make the walls appear to recede, but tart lemon yellow on the bedspread adds a refreshing zing of color.

In this condominium of only 1,500 square feet, rooms are alive with color, texture, and distinctive character suitable for displaying a fine collection of art. Although it's not an open floor plan, it has many of the same attributes because architecturally interesting walls, see-through display shelves, and other openings lead the eye from room to room, stretching the view to create a feeling of space.

Warm-tone plastered finishes and honey-color wood on floors, walls, shelves, and cabinets create a cocoon of color and texture, yet the comfortable furnishings are almost all neutral white. Replacing a few pillows, changing the rug, or rearranging the art revives the color scheme and creates a whole new look, preventing the monotony that often comes from living with the same furnishings for a long time.

OPEN AND CLOSED There's no such thing as a flat wall in this house, also shown on *pages 138–139*. Walls go from thin to thick and cabinets recess or extend to offer a dynamic interplay of space. The eye never rests as it lands on deep eggplant plaster, travels through openings in the walls, and catches sight of light patterns and the art that hangs at eye level in adjoining rooms. It is this constant push-pull movement that adds interest and keeps the house from feeling too confining.

▶ *MORE SURFACE Use space at the end of a cabinet to extend an extra counter into the kitchen. Even if it's only a foot or so across, you can use it as a breakfast bar, an extra serving surface, or even a food preparation center. It's also a good place for guests or children to sit and talk while you cook.*

VERTICAL SHELVING
Thick slabs of cherry wood form floating shelves that display art in the dining room and hall. Recessed fixtures in the ceiling focus attention on the art and also create scallops of light on the plastered walls for an interesting visual effect that relieves the eye from too much sameness. The central kitchen has a number of openings, such as this one over the sink, which create the illusion of having more space in adjoining rooms too. Notice that the top of the dining room table folds out to accommodate a larger crowd whenever necessary.

PRINCIPLES AT WORK

▶ **COLOR AND PATTERN** Beautifully patterned natural wood is a predominant surface in every room, appearing as flooring throughout the house and on walls, cabinets, and shelves too. Other pattern is kept to a minimum so as not to distract from the art. A wall wrapping around the centrally located kitchen is finished in eggplant-color plaster that has been waxed and polished to play up its texture. Most of the furniture has neutral upholstery, which is set off in the living room by a thick Oriental carpet in a multitude of colors.

▶ **ARRANGEMENT AND SCALE** A small round table in the kitchen contrasts with the angular elements in the room. Most other furniture is large in scale, especially in the living room where the few pieces that are used cluster around the fireplace.

▶ **STORAGE** Two unifying elements also function as storage space—the floating cherry shelves that reclaim formerly wasted corners and the routed wooden cabinets that are so prominent in the central portion of the house.

▶ **ILLUSION** Liberating the eye from the confines of four walls is a primary goal, achieved by openings in the walls and above the cabinets to allow a view of adjoining rooms. A glass-top coffee table plus shelves and a bath countertop that appear to float create the illusion of lightness.

▶ **BETTER USE OF SPACE** Walls have depth because portions have recesses for shelves or cabinets. Even the toilet is set into an indentation that adds definition and frees up an extra few inches of floor space.

TAKING IN THE VIEW *[left]*
Cabinets stop just short of the ceiling, and open shelves or pass-throughs extend the view into other rooms. One of the main unifying elements in this house is the generous use of wood for walls, cabinets, and floors. The round breakfast table tucks into a corner of the kitchen, while more formal meals take place in the dining room.

DRAMATIC BUT COZY *[opposite]*
A sandblasted concrete fireplace, an Oriental rug, and soft fabrics such as velvet pillows and a fringed throw add texture to this small living room. Used in several rooms, floating cherry shelves display artwork and books, converting a slim column of corner space into useful storage. The glass-top table and a clear acrylic frame on the art disappear, enlarging the sense of space.

▶ **SIMPLIFY** *Edit your accessories to achieve the clean and uncluttered look necessary for this type of house. This doesn't necessarily mean getting rid of things; it does mean storing most of them and rotating periodically to display only a few at a time.*

SHINY SURFACES [*opposite*]
The glass counter and a mirrored wall offer ample opportunity for reflection in the beech-paneled bath. Rising from the cabinet on silvery chrome legs, the counter almost appears to be floating in midair. A cabinet recessed in the wall and a vanity cabinet beneath the basin store items out of sight. The low-profile toilet tank is recessed in an alcove with a top that lines up with the counter for symmetry.

SLIDING STORAGE [*right*] A pull-out rack puts a few extra inches beside the closet to good use, providing easy access and dust-free storage for shoes. Floor-to-ceiling closets hold other built-in units as well as hanging bars for clothing. The back of the closet unit is the wall to the right of the bathroom sink (the recessed area goes into the back of the closet).

▶ **HANDY ACCESS** *Hang a shallow storage cabinet perpendicular to the bathroom mirror; choose one with mirrored doors to make the room seem larger. Or find a decorative piece with open shelves and let it sit on the counter to keep toiletries close at hand.*

A move to a smaller house sometimes necessitates a change of scale, as large furniture and oversize patterns that were perfect for another home suddenly seem too bold. Acquiescing to the reduced scale of the rooms, fine antiques and soft colors make peace with the size of the modest house. With an emphasis on comfortable but small-scale upholstered seating and mid-1800s wooden pieces, downsized furniture turns the dollhouse-size rooms into little jewels.

Color in the formal first floor is confined to neutral tones of chamois and pale apricot with subdued patterns, except for a sprinkling of dark accents to add punch and keep it from being bland. Collections include objects made of antique horn, leather-bound books, and oil paintings in deeper tones that lend much-needed depth to the pastel rooms. In the basement family room, butter-color walls, white woodwork, and blue and white accents drawn from antique transferware enliven the gentle palette.

In this home quilted fabrics, linen slipcovers, sisal carpeting, and restrained use of color create an up-to-date, timeless effect very much in harmony with the snug little house.

CHARMING COTTAGE [above]
Landscaped with low shrubs that anchor without hiding, this neat clapboard cottage is proof that a house doesn't have to be large to be attractive. Even on the outside there are elements of interest that distract from the small size— window boxes and a pair of stately planters by the front door hint at the refined style of the interior. The door opens into the living room, creating a mandatory traffic pattern without cutting through the furniture grouping.

SUBTLE SYMMETRY [opposite]
Not distracted by color, the eye is free to examine the interesting antique accessories dotting this tiny living room. Classic linen fabrics with dressmaker details create a quiet and refined ambience. The balloon shade at ceiling height makes the window seem taller, and the table skirt hides storage beneath it. Wall-to-wall sisal carpeting unifies the house in an unbroken flow of color and texture.

▶ **MULTIPLE WAYS** *Repetition of a shape is an excellent way to unify a room or even an entire house and make it seem more cohesive. The shape can be repeated in different forms—the balloon shade, table topper, and trefoil ottoman, for instance, all have scalloped edges— as long as they are related enough to be recognized as such.*

SMALL-SCALE FURNISHINGS
[opposite] Diminutive pieces of furniture do the jobs that built-ins in other houses might do. The antique bamboo bookcase holds a collection of leather-bound books, and a butler's tray is well-stocked as a bar for serving guests. When topped with a tray, the trefoil ottoman is used as a table.

CHANGE OF PACE *[left]* Dressed in pale slipcovers like other pieces in the house, the downstairs furniture has little color to arrest the eye. Its scale is small; a love seat takes the place of a full-size sofa. Blue print pillows and a custom-made ottoman/table draw their color from a collection of blue and white china.

▶ **STYLISH TREATMENT** *The slipcovered look is très chic these days, whether you have a cottage or another style of home. Update mismatched or hand-me-down furniture with natural or solid-color slipcovers or use a coordinating print for the back cushions. It's easy to remove covers for cleaning, which is a plus in households with pets or young children.*

PRINCIPLES AT WORK

▶ **COLOR AND PATTERN** Quiet colors, neutral walls, and sisal carpeting create a subdued and nonintrusive color scheme that allows the antique accessories to hold their own in the room and even shine. Pattern is confined to tone-on-tone designs, except for one leopard-print chair, accented because it is a favorite antique piece.

▶ **ARRANGEMENT AND SCALE** The extremely small size of this house directly determines the scale of every piece of furniture used. Reduced-size seating and scaled-down tables serve the function of larger but fewer pieces.

▶ **STORAGE** The best storage comes from the cabinets and shelves added to the basement family room. Doors hide items inside the large base cabinets and adjustable shelves backed by yellow walls display porcelain and books.

▶ **ILLUSION** A balloon shade in the living room disguises the window that is too short because the top of the shade goes all the way up to the ceiling. In the same room a floor-length cloth hides items kept beneath the round table.

▶ **CONVERSIONS** A dark and almost windowless basement room becomes a sunny family room with yellow paint, comfortable furniture, and elegantly trimmed storage cabinets.

▶ **BETTER USE OF SPACE** In the family room, ceiling-height storage cabinets create more square feet of shelf space than they take up in floor space. A love seat takes up less room than a sofa downstairs. Wall-hung cabinets store ironstone pieces in the kitchen.

ADDED STORAGE *[left]* With collections all over the house, the low-ceiling, windowless basement had to do its part in storing them. Banks of well-lit bookshelves, backed by buttery yellow walls, add much-needed light and display favorite antiques. Enclosed cabinets provide ample storage space. Sisal carpet, continued from upstairs, expands the apparent space by creating an unbroken surface on the floor.

KITCHEN COLLECTION *[above]* A collection of ironstone and Staffordshire finds a home in the kitchen, where there's a more relaxed version of the formality found in the rest of the house. Off-white woodwork and chamois walls continue from the living room, but honey-color pine in an antique door and a couple of kitchen tables warms the room. Overall, though, the scale is small and color is still limited.

With antiques, art, and ambience, this condo makes the case that a small space doesn't have to be bland. Deep, jewel-tone colors, touchable fabrics, textured walls, and a wealth of exotic accessories combine to create richly furnished rooms, yet a closer look reveals that basic space-enhancing principles are still at work. As you look at each room, note how each one flows into the next, with elements that repeat over and over in different forms as the eye travels from place to place. See how a steady hand with color and a commitment to unadorned window treatments, similar surface textures, classic furniture shapes, and built-in storage units skillfully create a backdrop for opulent accessories. The interplay between opposites—plain and fancy, or antique and contemporary—creates a dynamic that keeps the eye moving and interested.

PRIVATE GALLERY *[above]*
The bold, outgoing color in the entrance hall immediately introduces the dramatic color scheme of the house. The hall is both a passageway and a gallery that displays well-chosen paintings meant to be appreciated up close. Golden frames repeat the metallic tone of the glass-top brass table, a visually lightweight piece that takes up little apparent space. A track light fixture runs the length of the hall to throw light on each painting. The mellow oak parquet flooring and deep crown molding extend into adjoining rooms as unifying elements.

FRAMED VIEW *[opposite]*
The interior hallway doesn't have a window, but an impressive mirror does a good job of simulating one, opening up the room. Centering the table and mirror in front of the cased opening between rooms creates the effect of a second frame, focusing even more attention on the mirror. The opening also allows an unimpeded view of the deep crown molding, an important decorative element that draws attention upward.

REPEATING AN ELEMENT

Repetition of elements plays a large part in the decorating success of this house by acting as a bridge, beckoning the curious eye to travel out of one room and into the adjoining rooms. Consider the use of metallic accents: In every room metallics drawn from the Chinese screen in the living room are echoed in brass table bases, lamps, mirror frames, hardware, tabletop accessories, upholstery tacks, a towel cart, and other items. All share the golden gleam that ties the space together and, with the rich and touchable fabrics, creates a feeling of opulence throughout the house. Deep color plus black, mellow wood tones, Eastern or classically influenced accessories, and elaborate crown moldings are also repeated in different rooms.

PRINCIPLES AT WORK

▶ **COLOR AND PATTERN** A strict hand with color isn't synonymous with drabness. By limiting the colors of walls, floors, and fabrics to wood tones, shades of metallic gold, golden beige, cinnabar red, and jolts of black for emphasis, the palette throughout the house works together as each room flows into another. Grass-cloth wallcovering adds textural interest while offering a noncompeting background for furnishings.

▶ **ARRANGEMENT AND SCALE** The furniture is arranged in conversational groupings and the large rug announces which part is reserved as the living room. The circular placement of the living room furniture offers access, yet routes traffic smoothly between that area and the dining room.

▶ **ILLUSION** Wooden blinds in a tone similar to the cabinetry take up almost no visual space. The tall screen and multipiece crown moldings accented with the wall color draw attention to the top of the room; other furnishings are kept below waist level, resulting in more apparent distance between the two heights. The beveled glass coffee table almost disappears.

▶ **STORAGE** The entire length of the room is one giant storage area, wrapping the window in a frame of shelves and cabinets. Floor-to-ceiling bookcases, deep enough for two rows of books or for placing items out of sight behind the books, have double the usual storage capacity. Cabinets with solid doors store anything that needs to be hidden from view. Another large unit also serves as a bar. The big bonus—these storage walls require minimum square footage along the edges of the room where traffic between areas never goes anyway.

▶ **MULTIPURPOSE FURNITURE** One storage cabinet serves as a buffet for entertaining. The bathroom sink has a skirt that covers bath necessities stored underneath it.

▶ **VERTICAL ACCENTS** *Lead the eye upward, even if your room lacks impressive crown molding, by including such elements as tree-size houseplants, vases of tall twigs, stacked paintings, and floor-to-ceiling draperies.*

CONVIVIAL ROUND [*opposite*]
Varying numbers of guests can crowd around the large round table, yet it always seems the right size because chairs line up on the wall if not needed. The storage wall running the length of the room wraps the window with ceiling-height bookcases and spacious storage cabinets. Capped with a finished top, the ledge comes into its own when it serves as a buffet for dinner parties, but it displays favorite pieces of art at other times. Draperies would have been too bulky to use on the surrounded window, but slim shades provide light control and also privacy.

LIGHT ENTERTAINMENT [*right*]
More shelving and a glass-top cabinet that serves as a bar share the rich wood tones, fluted moldings, and brass pulls of other cabinetry in the room. Plate-glass mirrors behind the bar and behind the glass doors create the illusion of seeing through the cabinets and into the next room, increasing apparent space. Tying the whole room together, deep crown molding surrounds the perimeter.

LIGHT BUT NO VIEW [above left]
The kitchen opens directly off the living room/dining room—a convenient feature for serving but not at all desirable if the kitchen is messy. Double doors are a good solution: They're often left open for a more spacious feeling in both rooms, but when they are closed, glass panes admit light while shirred panels of sheer fabric obscure the view.

HIDEAWAY OFFICE [above right]
The small closet is nevertheless large enough to contain a well-equipped office. Storage cabinets, corner shelving, and a file basket on casters organize books and paperwork, and a rolling office chair allows instant movement from computer to paperwork. When the office isn't in use, double doors close to hide its contents from view.

COMELY COVER-UPS [opposite]
Sumptuous fabric drapes each side of the tub to create a private alcove that blends with the style of other rooms. The floor-to-ceiling drapery panels slide on rods behind a cornice of crown molding that continues unbroken around the room. A tailored skirt, attached to the basin with hook-and-loop tape for easy removal, hides bath essentials stored behind it.

▶ *TWO HALVES Convert a solid-core door into two double doors by cutting it down the center. Finish the cut edges and hinge each door. Add molding to one side to hide any gap between the closed doors.*

Unusual accessories, interesting textures, and an eye for display set this house apart, but it takes the artful application of space-expanding tricks to make the rooms seem larger than they really are.

In every room accents near the ceiling draw the eye upward, breaking through the artificial cap that exists just above eye level to include the abundant space near the ceiling. The lower half is also filled with substantial furniture and objects that demand attention. The eye continually moves from high to low and back again, receiving the impression that the available space is plentiful. Reflective surfaces also make rooms seem larger—in the dining room, for instance, the glass table disappears, and there's a whole wall of mirrors that function like windows to maximize light and views.

Unifying elements include calming walls and rich wood flooring, and each room repeats decorative motifs or colors used in adjoining rooms. Some rooms even borrow space from each other: When the entrance hall buffet is used for serving, the adjoining dining room expands to include that area too. As you look at this house, observe these principles in action and see how they help the house live large.

ON THE DIAGONAL *[left]* Seeing furniture pulled away from the walls and placed at angles is a good tip-off that it's arranged to create the illusion of more space. Although the main pieces still cluster around the fireplace, there is now room to spare behind them. Other space expanders include a mirror above the mantel, window treatments mounted near the ceiling, and tall plants and vertical columns that draw even more attention to the top of the room. The area rug adds a dash of color to accent the floor, and the eye takes it all in—moving from one element to another and relaying its impression that the area is larger than it really is.

▶ **PARTY DRESS** Make temporary slipcovers to cover dining room chairs or to unify chairs that are only occasionally used for dining. These slipcovers are long panels of lined fabric with ties sewn at strategic points so they can be put on or removed easily.

PRINCIPLES AT WORK

▶ **COLOR AND PATTERN** Walls are subdued, floors are dark wood, and most of the color comes from rugs and the rich fabrics that grace upholstered pieces. Pattern is sparse except in the dining room draperies, but there's an abundance of texture throughout the house.

▶ **ARRANGEMENT AND SCALE** Placing the furniture at a slight diagonal in the living room means that there's space behind it, space that's put to work holding plants, columns, and other tall accessories.

▶ **STORAGE** Large furniture stores some items in the rooms where they are needed, but built-ins accomplish the rest—two bookcases tuck into the space beneath the windows flanking the fireplace. Pretty china becomes a decorative element because the storage cabinets have see-through glass doors. The floor-length cloth in the living room covers hidden storage space beneath the table.

▶ **ILLUSION** There's an interaction of big and little, large and small, and especially high (ceiling) and low (floors) that keeps the eye moving and makes the space seem larger. An accent on vertical elements and ceiling-height entryways opens up the rooms too. Mirrors are a major element, reflecting light from windows and artificial sources and doubling the space they reflect.

▶ **CONVERSIONS** The entrance hall buffet is a workhorse piece of furniture, used for display, storage, and serving meals. Mismatched chairs wear stylish slipcovers that unite them in a gentle rainbow of harmonious shades drawn from the draped windows.

▶ **BETTER USE OF SPACE** Some adjoining rooms borrow space from each other because large openings or doors allow an almost effortless flow of traffic between them. The dining room takes space from the entrance hall when the buffet is used for serving food, and the deck outside seems like a continuation of the kitchen.

MIRROR, MIRROR [opposite] Multiple reflections going all the way up to the ceiling create the effect of extra windows on the wall, amplifying the daylight coming through the real window. At night the mirrors reflect the glow of the candlelight fixture above the table. The round glass table easily accommodates a crowd—if an extra seat is added at the last minute, another tie-on party slipcover can easily be added so it harmonizes with other chairs.

HARDWORKING PIECE [above] The entrance hall buffet acts as a hall table, stores large serving pieces, and is sometimes used for serving, which enlarges the dining room to include hallway space. The paintings are arranged so that one focuses attention upward while the pair at the bottom has visual weight that anchors the group. The whole vignette, along with the buffet, forms an arrow shape pointing up. The eye, of course, is not aware of being subtly directed, but it follows the direction of the arrow, taking in more space at a glance and making the room appear larger.

DUST-FREE DISPLAY *[above left]*
Extra sets of pretty china find a
home in wall-mounted cabinets
with clear glass doors. They're
arranged for display, but if there's
a need for more compact storage,
translucent or patterned glass is
easy to substitute. Base cabinets
are handy for storage and the top
can be used for serving.

OUTDOOR ROOM *[above right]*
Single-pane French doors provide
an unobstructed view of the
outdoors, allowing the eye to
travel from kitchen to deck with
no break. Likewise the two areas
are on one level—guests wander
from one to the other and get the
benefit of the extra space right
outside the doors.

SPARE CORNER *[opposite]* An
ornate wall-mounted table with
open space beneath it displays
architectural fragments that echo
its neoclassical style. A swoop of
gauzy fabric softens the blinds
without seeming too heavy, while
a mirror expands the space and
adds light. Bold-color flowers
accent the all-neutral scheme.

▶ *VERTICAL ACCENTS Hang small paintings and objects on a narrow wall to form a column, ending near*
the ceiling. Or stack two larger paintings directly above each other, creating a vertical element to draw the
eye upward and create the illusion of space.

When planning your room schemes on paper, use the symbols here and on the following pages to profile your spaces and visualize them with more dimension. Here's how to use the paper kit:

▶ **1. Copy pages 185–190** on a black and white copy machine at a local copy shop. Make several copies of the graph paper for different scenarios. Or on plain paper, trace only the templates that best reflect your furnishings. Then use the graph on pages 189–190 to begin experimenting with different arrangements.

▶ **2. Measure your room.** Plot it on the grid, using one square per square foot of floor space. Determine the length of each wall and draw it onto the floor plan. Mark windows with a double line, leave an open area for doorways, and indicate door swings. Include architectural features such as fireplaces, sliding glass doors, and stairways.

▶ **3. Measure your present furniture pieces** or the new ones you plan to purchase. Match them to the corresponding kit symbols and cut out the templates.

▶ **4. Find a focal point.** Physically, this is the cornerstone around which you'll group your furnishings; visually, it's the dramatic element that draws you into a room. If your room doesn't have a natural focus—a fireplace, built-in bookcases, or an expansive window—substitute a large-scale or boldly colored accessory or use freestanding wall units.

▶ **5. Once you've found the focus**, arrange your furniture templates on the graph-paper floor plan.

▶ **6. When you arrive at an arrangement** you'd like to save for future reference, tape down the pieces with transparent tape and tuck the plan into your style file.

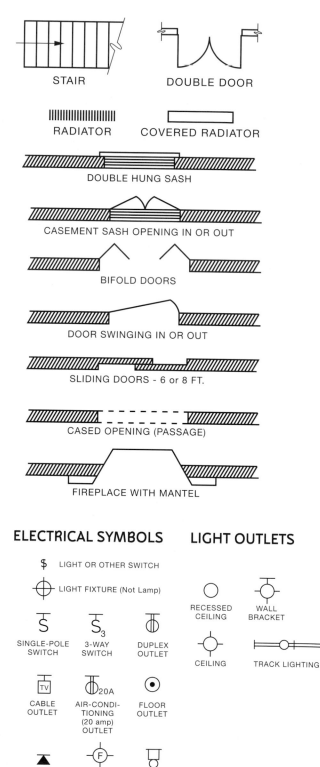

ARCHITECTURAL SYMBOLS

STAIR DOUBLE DOOR

RADIATOR COVERED RADIATOR

DOUBLE HUNG SASH

CASEMENT SASH OPENING IN OR OUT

BIFOLD DOORS

DOOR SWINGING IN OR OUT

SLIDING DOORS - 6 or 8 FT.

CASED OPENING (PASSAGE)

FIREPLACE WITH MANTEL

ELECTRICAL SYMBOLS

$ LIGHT OR OTHER SWITCH

LIGHT FIXTURE (Not Lamp)

SINGLE-POLE SWITCH

3-WAY SWITCH

DUPLEX OUTLET

CABLE OUTLET

AIR-CONDI-TIONING (20 amp) OUTLET

FLOOR OUTLET

TELEPHONE CEILING FAN BELL

LIGHT OUTLETS

RECESSED CEILING

WALL BRACKET

CEILING

TRACK LIGHTING

UPHOLSTERED FURNITURE & BEDDING

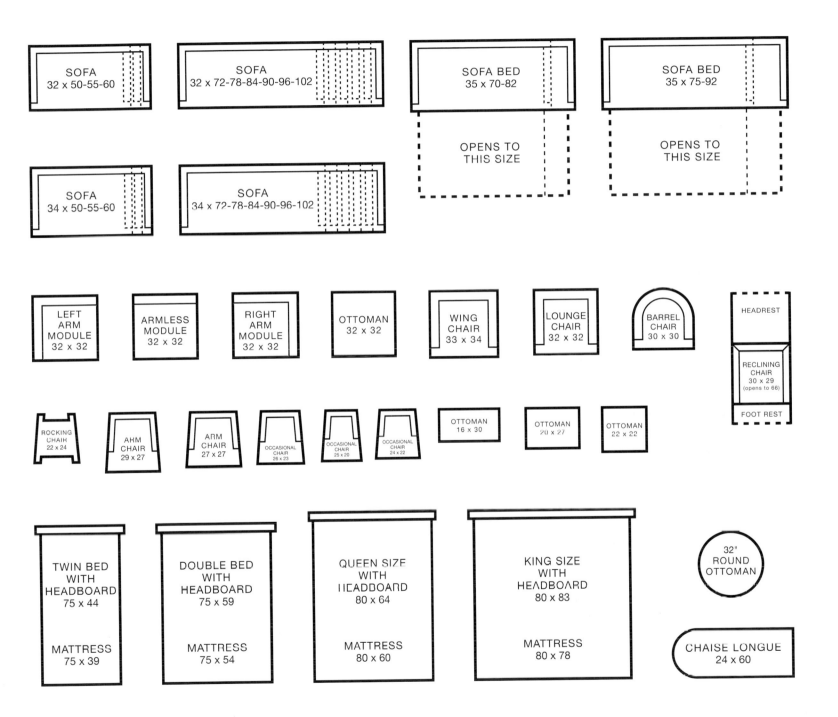

SOFA
32 x 50-55-60

SOFA
32 x 72-78-84-90-96-102

SOFA BED
35 x 70-82

OPENS TO
THIS SIZE

SOFA BED
35 x 75-92

OPENS TO
THIS SIZE

SOFA
34 x 50-55-60

SOFA
34 x 72-78-84-90-96-102

LEFT
ARM
MODULE
32 x 32

ARMLESS
MODULE
32 x 32

RIGHT
ARM
MODULE
32 x 32

OTTOMAN
32 x 32

WING
CHAIR
33 x 34

LOUNGE
CHAIR
32 x 32

BARREL
CHAIR
30 x 30

HEADREST

RECLINING
CHAIR
30 x 29
(opens to 66)

FOOT REST

ROCKING
CHAIR
22 x 24

ARM
CHAIR
29 x 27

ARM
CHAIR
27 x 27

OCCASIONAL
CHAIR
26 x 23

OCCASIONAL
CHAIR
25 x 20

OCCASIONAL
CHAIR
24 x 22

OTTOMAN
16 x 30

OTTOMAN
20 x 27

OTTOMAN
22 x 22

TWIN BED
WITH
HEADBOARD
75 x 44

MATTRESS
75 x 39

DOUBLE BED
WITH
HEADBOARD
75 x 59

MATTRESS
75 x 54

QUEEN SIZE
WITH
HEADBOARD
80 x 64

MATTRESS
80 x 60

KING SIZE
WITH
HEADBOARD
80 x 83

MATTRESS
80 x 78

32"
ROUND
OTTOMAN

CHAISE LONGUE
24 x 60

OCCASIONAL TABLES & SPECIAL PIECES

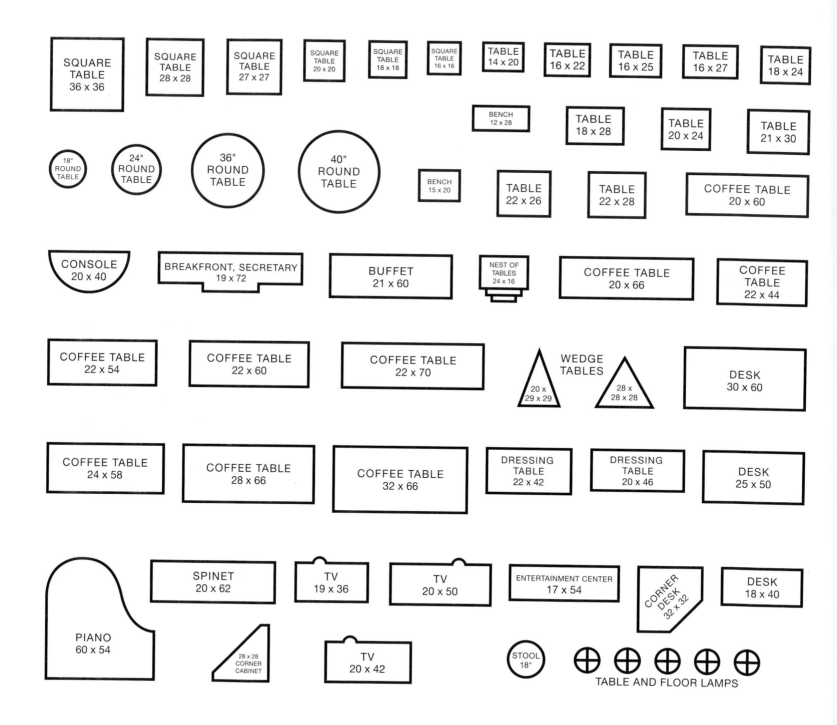

SQUARE TABLE 36 x 36

SQUARE TABLE 28 x 28

SQUARE TABLE 27 x 27

SQUARE TABLE 20 x 20

SQUARE TABLE 18 x 18

SQUARE TABLE 16 x 16

TABLE 14 x 20

TABLE 16 x 22

TABLE 16 x 25

TABLE 16 x 27

TABLE 18 x 24

BENCH 12 x 28

TABLE 18 x 28

TABLE 20 x 24

TABLE 21 x 30

18" ROUND TABLE

24" ROUND TABLE

36" ROUND TABLE

40" ROUND TABLE

BENCH 15 x 20

TABLE 22 x 26

TABLE 22 x 28

COFFEE TABLE 20 x 60

CONSOLE 20 x 40

BREAKFRONT, SECRETARY 19 x 72

BUFFET 21 x 60

NEST OF TABLES 24 x 16

COFFEE TABLE 20 x 66

COFFEE TABLE 22 x 44

COFFEE TABLE 22 x 54

COFFEE TABLE 22 x 60

COFFEE TABLE 22 x 70

WEDGE TABLES

20 x 29 x 29

28 x 28 x 28

DESK 30 x 60

COFFEE TABLE 24 x 58

COFFEE TABLE 28 x 66

COFFEE TABLE 32 x 66

DRESSING TABLE 22 x 42

DRESSING TABLE 20 x 46

DESK 25 x 50

SPINET 20 x 62

TV 19 x 36

TV 20 x 50

ENTERTAINMENT CENTER 17 x 54

CORNER DESK 32 x 32

DESK 18 x 40

PIANO 60 x 54

28 x 28 CORNER CABINET

TV 20 x 42

STOOL 18"

TABLE AND FLOOR LAMPS

DINING TABLES & CHAIRS

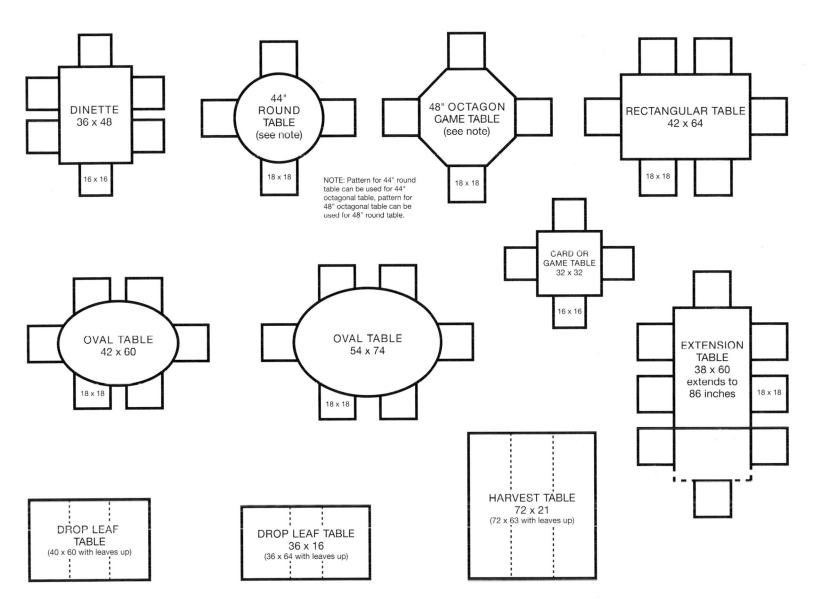

DINETTE
36 x 48

16 x 16

44"
ROUND
TABLE
(see note)

18 x 18

48" OCTAGON
GAME TABLE
(see note)

18 x 18

NOTE: Pattern for 44" round
table can be used for 44"
octagonal table, pattern for
48" octagonal table can be
used for 48" round table.

RECTANGULAR TABLE
42 x 64

18 x 18

OVAL TABLE
42 x 60

18 x 18

OVAL TABLE
54 x 74

18 x 18

CARD OR
GAME TABLE
32 x 32

16 x 16

EXTENSION
TABLE
38 x 60
extends to
86 inches

18 x 18

HARVEST TABLE
72 x 21
(72 x 63 with leaves up)

DROP LEAF
TABLE
(40 x 60 with leaves up)

DROP LEAF TABLE
36 x 16
(36 x 64 with leaves up)

STORAGE PIECES & OTHER SPECIAL PIECES

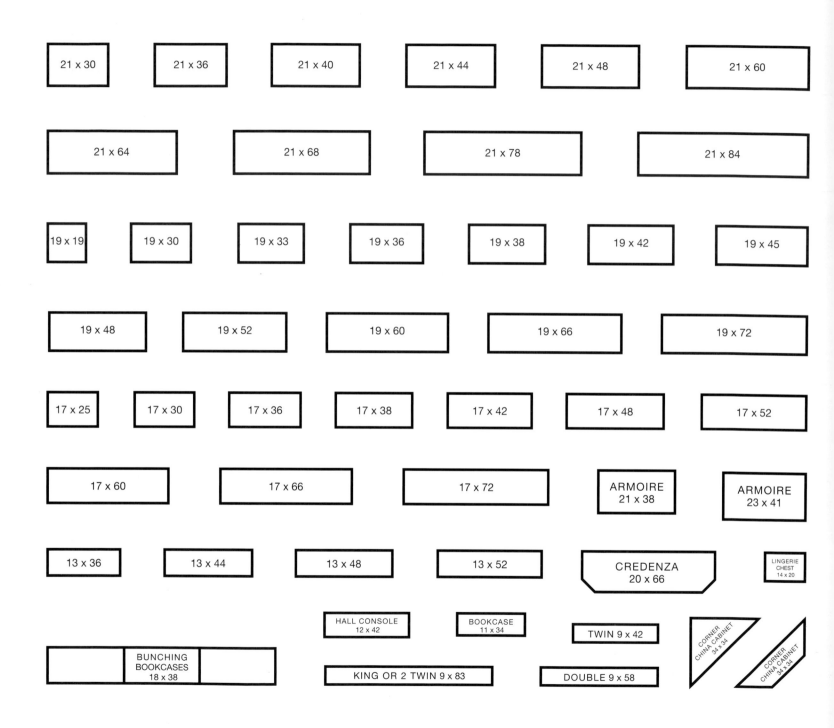

21 x 30 · 21 x 36 · 21 x 40 · 21 x 44 · 21 x 48 · 21 x 60

21 x 64 · 21 x 68 · 21 x 78 · 21 x 84

19 x 19 · 19 x 30 · 19 x 33 · 19 x 36 · 19 x 38 · 19 x 42 · 19 x 45

19 x 48 · 19 x 52 · 19 x 60 · 19 x 66 · 19 x 72

17 x 25 · 17 x 30 · 17 x 36 · 17 x 38 · 17 x 42 · 17 x 48 · 17 x 52

17 x 60 · 17 x 66 · 17 x 72 · ARMOIRE 21 x 38 · ARMOIRE 23 x 41

13 x 36 · 13 x 44 · 13 x 48 · 13 x 52 · CREDENZA 20 x 66 · LINGERIE CHEST 14 x 20

HALL CONSOLE 12 x 42 · BOOKCASE 11 x 34 · TWIN 9 x 42 · CORNER CHINA CABINET 34 x 34

BUNCHING BOOKCASES 18 x 38 · KING OR 2 TWIN 9 x 83 · DOUBLE 9 x 58 · CORNER CHINA CABINET 34 x 34

1 SQUARE = 1 FOOT

1 SQUARE = 1 FOOT

▶ **A-B**

Accessories
   accent colors, 11, 12, 145
   as focal points, 12, 22, 83, 94, 133, 151, 170
   rotating, 160
   vertical/horizontal accents, 26–27, 181
Adjoining rooms
   openings, 52–53, 55, 145, 159–160, 170, 181
   repetition, 16, 17, 173
   using color, 8, 12, 149, 154
   wide openings, 52, 55
Art placement, 26, 28, 94, 130, 133, 145
Attic rooms, 46, 71, 113, 134
Bathrooms, 70–71, 118–120, 146, 152, 176
Bedrooms, 108–113, 134
Benches, 34, 72, 91, 105, 116
Bookcases, 26, 62–63, 72, 169, 175, 181
Breakfast nook, 24, 91, 105

▶ **C**

Cabinets, 26, 34, 76, 149, 182
Carpeting. *See* Rugs
Ceilings, 26, 77, 100, 142
Child's room, 67, 72, 114–117
Closet space
   as bathroom, 70–71, 163
   craft storage, 66
   as display cabinet, 130
   as office, home, 34, 176
   pantry, 33
   portable, 58
Color
   accent, 11, 12, 15, 28, 140, 145, 173
   basics, 8–15
   in child's room, 115
   contemporary style, 156
   cottage style, 164, 168
   in dining area, 91
   eclectic style, 178
   elegant style, 170, 173
   in kitchens, 99, 152
   in living rooms, 80, 83, 86, 151
   modern style, 140, 145
   neutral palettes, 11, 12, 15, 86, 164
   neutrals plus one, 12, 15, 83
   one color rooms, 11, 142, 145
   traditional style, 148, 154–155
   white/pale colors, 12, 140, 142, 145
Columns, 26, 52, 83, 179
Contemporary style, 156–163
Conversions, 46, 58–67, 130, 168
Corners, 125, 160, 182
Cottage style, 164–169
Countertops, 33, 106, 107

▶ **D-E**

Dining area, 88–97, 159
Display areas
   closet conversion, 130
   in dining area, 94, 159
   in kitchens, 33, 99, 107, 182
   photo, 76
   stairway, 133
   in workstations, 122
Doors
   disguised, 31, 34
   French, 55, 67, 182
   glass, 37, 40, 42, 43, 53, 71, 80, 105, 176
   sliding, 145
Eclectic style, 178–183
Elegant style, 170–177
Exercise room, 60

▶ **F-I**

Fabric
   patterns, 15–18, 85
   texture, 145, 160
   toile, 17
   unifying area, 18
Fireplace, 23, 34, 49, 149, 151, 160, 179
Furniture
   in child's room, 114–117
   color, 11, 12, 46
   concealing defects, 46
   multiuse, 65, 96, 140, 154, 173, 181
   in office, home, 125
   outdoor, 146
   patterns, 15–18, 85
   scale/visual weight, 24, 86, 149, 164, 167, 168
   shape, 164
Furniture arrangement
   angled, 21, 22, 23, 154, 179, 181
   basics, 20–27, 52, 145
   structural limitations, 109
   traffic patterns, 21, 86, 134, 173
Greenhouse, indoor, 44
Hobby/craft room, 66–67, 127, 129
Illusion, 38–57, 145, 154, 159, 168, 173, 181
Islands, 68–69, 102–103, 142

▶ **K-L**

Kitchens, 98–107, 125, 142
   color, 152
   overhead storage/display, 100, 107
   storage, 33, 68–69, 72, 154
Laundry, 57, 60, 126–127
Light
   in bathroom, 71, 119
   in bedroom, 109, 113
   lighting types, 43

in living rooms, 80, 85
natural, 15, 53, 74–75, 105, 142, 145, 154
for painting, 67
skylight, 67, 100, 119
task, 42, 43
using mirrors, 40–41, 119, 133, 154–155, 181
Living rooms, 11, 80–87, 151

▶ **M-O**

Mirrors
in bathroom, 70, 71, 118–119, 163
expanding space, 34, 38, 40, 152, 170, 175, 179, 182
hiding television, 49, 83
as light reflectors, 40–41, 133, 154–155, 181
lining cabinets, 31, 130, 175
as window treatments, 74
Modern style, 140–147
Moldings, 27, 83, 85, 94, 170, 173, 175, 176
Office, home, 46, 122–125, 127, 176
Ottoman, 64, 83, 86, 149, 154, 167

▶ **P-R**

Paint
on ceilings, 26, 77
chalkboard, 67
color, 8, 142
on furniture, 11, 12, 46
trompe l'oeil, 56–57
Patterns, 15–18, 85
Pegs, 137, 145, 146
Room dividers/partitions, 44, 60, 92, 107, 134
Rugs, 20, 21, 26, 80, 145, 169, 173, 179

▶ **S**

Screens
Chinese, 173
fixed half screen, 92
outdoor, 146
shoji, 48, 92
sliding, 92
Shelving
in bathroom, 70, 121, 154

built-in, 28, 67, 80, 86, 94, 169, 175
in dining area, 94, 96
floor-to-ceiling, 27, 60
glass, 41, 53, 74
in kitchens, 68, 99, 100, 107, 154
shallow/recessed, 31, 33, 37, 70, 94, 159, 163
window shelf, 74–75, 88, 91
in workshop, 129
Sink
in child's room, 116
skirt, 176
Slipcovers, 11, 46, 145, 167, 180, 181
Space-expanders, 68–77. *See also* Mirrors
in bathroom, 118–119
in bedroom, 145
glass doors, 43, 145
recessed shelving. *See* Shelving
window pass-through, 53
Spice racks, 33, 37, 102
Stairway walls, 60, 133
Storage
aids, 100, 111, 127
backdoor, 37, 137
basics, 28–37, 145
in bathroom, 70, 76, 121, 152, 154
under bed, 37, 111
in bedroom, 109, 113
bench, 34, 72, 91, 105
in child's room, 115, 116
cubes, 63, 72, 94, 111, 116
in dining area, 94
in hobby/craft/paint room, 66, 129
islands, 68–69, 102–103
in kitchens, 33, 68–69, 72, 100, 107, 154
in laundry, 126–127
in living rooms, 80, 86, 173
in office, home, 122
in stairwell, 33, 72, 122
wine, 37

▶ **T-V**

Tables
buffet, 181

faux leather, 149
glass tops, 46, 85, 140, 160, 170, 181
multiuse, 64–65
round, 65, 91, 96, 175
space saving, 88
wall mounted, 182
Television, hidden, 48–51, 83
Traditional style, 148–155
Traffic patterns
in bedroom, 111
in kitchens, 106
using dividing wall, 134
zones, 20, 21, 86
Vertical/horizontal elements
accessories, 182
arches, 85
basics, 26–27, 83, 174
columns, 26, 52, 83, 179
curtain rods, 45
mirrors, 119
moldings, 170, 173

▶ **W-Z**

Wall treatments
color, 8–15, 140, 148, 156
faux views, 56–57
glass, 111, 119
knee walls, 113
patterns, 16–17
stenciling, 57
texture, 173
Window Treatments. *See also* Light
balloon shade, 164, 168
glass shelves, 74–75
minimal coverage, 44–45, 86, 142, 173, 175
window box, 75
Zones, 20–21, 86